ti

Recording the vision. Making it plain. That you may run.

This edition of
Blood Against Blood
is dedicated to those
brothers and sisters around the world who,
above all else, seek to walk as passionate,
authentic and trusting followers of Christ.

Walk On.

Blood Against Blood
Arthur Sydney Booth-Clibborn

The original of this the third edition of *Blood Against Blood* is in the library at Cornell University. There are no known copyright restrictions in the United States on the use of this text.

The author belonged to no partricular denomination of Christians, therefore none share the responsibility for the views expressed other than the author.

Foundation Press is the non-academic division of Foundation University Press.

Copies of this book may be ordered through booksellers or by contacting:

Foundation Press
Post Office Box 12429
1100 AK Amsterdam, The Netherlands

info@foundationuniversity.com
foundationuniversitypress.com

ISBN: 978-94-90179-12-0

cover illustration | *Fair Witness* by Christine M. Gilman   **design by** | timmyroland.com

Introduction

This book by Arthur Sidney Booth-Clibborn (1855-1939) that you now hold in your hands inspired me to reconsider my understanding of Jesus Christ and what it means to "take up the cross" and love my enemies. It was a historically powerful and influential book as it significantly affected the early peace witness of the early Pentecostal movement. It served as the clearest and strongest link between Quakerism and early Pentecostal pacifism and I think that it can inspire us still today in the twenty-first century as we seek be Spirit-empowered peacemakers and justice seekers.

"The Society of Friends," wrote Donald Green, "has produced so far only two systematic thinkers . . . Robert Barclay and Joseph John Gurney." Both of these authors, who wrote the most widely read and best known explanations and defenses of Quakerism, were ancestors of Arthur Sidney Booth-Clibborn. Robert Barclay penned An Apology for the True Christian Divinity as the Same is Held Forth and Preached by the People, in Scorn, Called Quakers in 1678 and Joseph John Gurney wrote Observations on the Religious Peculiarities of the Society of Friends in 1824. Voltaire lauded the former and the latter went through ten editions in England and America. When Booth-Clibborn states in Blood Against Blood that "ancestral examples . . . affected both my views and duties in this question of the two opposite kinds of war" his readers can be assured that he had been influenced by some of the greatest examples of Quakerism.

Booth-Clibborn's Quaker heritage began in the mid 1650s when John Clibborn tried to burn down a Quaker meetinghouse that had been erected on his land in Moate, Ireland. Instead, he converted to Quakerism because of the preaching of Thomas Lowe; Lowe also influenced William Penn to adopt Quaker peace principles. John Clibborn resigned his military position under Oliver Cromwell and harbored refugees during the wars that followed. "His life was attempted three times" because he was a Quaker but he would not testify against his enemies because "he bore them no ill-will."

During that same decade Colonel David Barclay, who was at one time the military governor over the majority of Scotland, "experience[ed] the new birth," renounced war as anti-Christian, and was accused of succumbing to "the scandalous errors [sic] of Quaquarism [sic]." John Greenleaf Whittier noted in both poetry and prose the persecutions suffered by David Barclay. His son Robert Barclay became the influential theologian and traveled with both George Fox and William Penn. Joseph John Gurney also descended from David Barclay and persuasively argued for the relevance and importance of Quakerism on a broad scale through public speaking and publishing.

Arthur Booth-Clibborn touts his female Quaker ancestors as wonderful examples of nonviolence and "prominent women ministers in the Society." He claimed that women in ministry encouraged peace, provided good role models, and that "the restoration of women's ministry to its normal place in the public service of Christ [would show] the unlawfulness of war for the Christian." This emphasis on women in leadership and ministry should continue to be at the forefront of our work for justice, as it has been shown repeatedly in empirical studies that as women lead and are empowered local communities are strengthened to a greater degree.

Arthur Sidney Booth-Clibborn valued his rich Quaker heritage and his acceptance of the holiness movement and the Pentecostal message only strengthened his pacifism. He considered himself a Quaker as well as a Pentecostal and wrote his book, Blood Against Blood, from the perspective of a Quaker missionary. He was "recorded" as a Quaker minister at an "unusually early age" and never drifted from those Quaker truths even while working with the Salvation Army, which he joined in 1881 at the age of twenty-six. In fact, twenty years later he left the Salvation Army over the issues of pacifism, healing, and premillennialism after General William Booth (founder of the Salvation Army) rejected his requests to preach the "full plain Gospel of the Sermon on the Mount." Dubbed the "apostle of abandonment," Booth-Clibborn spent time in jail in Switzerland and lived "under the sentence of death from the anarchists of five continental lands for over 10 years." While street preaching in 1905 an angry mob attacked him and pierced his leg with an iron bar. The resulting blood poisoning turned to gangrene and required four surgeries to save his life, but he never completely recovered.

Blood Against Blood was the first of two systematic presentations of Christian pacifism by Quaker Pentecostals. In it Booth-Clibborn encapsulates the Quaker arguments against war that were eventually adopted by the Assemblies of God and other Pentecostal denominations. He insists that absolute nonparticipation in war should be a Christian ethic, not just a Quaker one. He presents the two-fold premise of his book in the title. First, the blood of carnal warfare is opposite the blood of Christ and the two are "mutually excluding and never reconcilable." Second, the blood of Christ is the only power by which the blood of warfare could be overcome and conquered. "Christianity is the only remedy to war. Not a bloodless gospel on the one hand, not an adulterated evangelicalism on the other. It must be Blood against blood."

John Howard Yoder described Booth-Clibborn's kind of pacifism as that of "the virtuous minority" or "vocational pacifism." Christians were to live according to a different ethic than that which could be required of the rest of the world. This approach calls "into doubt this axiom that the same ethics are for everybody . . . all are invited to live on this level, but not all are expected or required to do so." This minority morality allowed the church to function according to its prophetic vocation without demanding that everybody else live the same way. He did not espouse Martin Ceadel's optimistic pacifism that hoped to change the world for good, but a 'pessimistic' pacifism that witnessed to truth in the painful and sinful interim. Booth-Clibborn was a faithful Quaker but he also appreciated, supported, and participated in the Pentecostal movement, "all their [he and his wife's] sympathies were with the Outpouring, even from the beginning. How could it be otherwise when nine of their children had received their Pentecost." Indeed, Arthur Booth-Clibborn himself received the "baptism in the Holy Spirit" under the ministry of a Quaker minister. His public endorsement of the

Pentecostal movement provided it with more respectability than it otherwise would have had, and he shared that Pentecostalism "reminds me of the days of early Quakerism, and of what one has known of the days of closest fellowship with the Crucified One." He even argued that the combination of Pentecostalism and pacifism formed an unbelievably powerful spiritual force. James Robinson noted that he maintained a "strong belief that acceptance of the pacifist and Pentecostal message by the [Salvation] Army would have returned it to its roots, to the time it was a spiritual force in the nation. . . ."

Arthur Booth-Clibborn's influence on early Pentecostalism came primarily from his book and numerous articles in The Pentecostal Evangel, but his children also had an impact. William Booth-Clibborn (d. 1969), the fifth child of Arthur Booth-Clibborn, was a charter member of the Assemblies of God in 1914 and wrote many books of his own. His 1936 work entitled The Baptism in the Holy Spirit: A Personal Testimony illustrates the close connection that his family, especially his pacifist father, had with the beginning of the Pentecostal movement. William Booth-Clibborn related several statements that his father made about the Pentecostal revival and experience. In reference to a woman at a mission hall Arthur wrote, "She is speaking by the Spirit and Power of God in a language unfamiliar to her. This is the unknown tongue you read about in Scripture. Is it not wonderful that God should be again baptizing with the Holy Ghost like He did in the early days of the Christian Church." Arthur Booth-Clibborn also "proclaimed to one and all that this [Pentecostal] revival was destined to sweep the world."

William Booth-Clibborn even claimed that "unless my parents had stepped out on questions of conscience and the advocacy of advanced truths such as . . . the anti-Christian character of all carnal warfare, we would never have been ready as a family to experience Pentecost in our home." This significant statement revealed the connection between Quaker pacifism and early Pentecostalism in the mind of at least this one founder of the Assemblies of God. It also revealed the connection between the baptism in the Holy Spirit and pacifism. For although pacifism preceded the baptism in the Holy Spirit as preparation through holiness, the Booth-Clibborns explained that the Holy Spirit provided the power to be nonviolent even in the face of hatred.

Three sons and two daughters of Arthur Booth-Clibborn also related to the Assemblies of God. Eric Booth-Clibborn was an Assemblies of God missionary who died shortly after reaching the French African Sudan. He wrote five articles for The Pentecostal Evangel and his wife wrote one as well. Samuel Herbert Booth-Clibborn wrote two articles against war that were published in 1917 in The Weekly Evangel. They reflected the arguments presented by his father in Blood Against Blood and were absolutely pacifistic. He also penned a book modeled after his father's that declared the same unquestionable ethic for Christians.

The early Assemblies of God leaders had great respect for Arthur Booth-Clibborn and his family. In 1915 The Weekly Evangel strongly recommended Blood Against Blood to all of its readers when E. N. Bell and J. R. Flower served as editors.

> *A most striking, realistic and forceful book by Arthur Sidney Booth-Clibborn, an English Pentecostal Evangelist and Elder who has put into words the principles burning in the hearts of all the Pentecostal saints on the subject of whether a Christian should go to war or not. This book presents war from a Christian standpoint and is not intended for those out of Christ. Should the United States go to war with Germany, or any other nation, what shall be the attitude of the Pentecostal people. Send for a copy of this wonderful book and then make a decision. Price 55 cts. Postpaid. The Gospel Publishing House. . . .*

Another advertisement lauded it by stating that "The Gospel Publishing House is in possession of a powerful book" and encouraged Pentecostals to "purchase it and become imbued with the spirit of its contents, in a complete opposition and protest against war and the shedding of blood." They were selling an edition replete with Quaker references, quotes, and an impressive account of Booth-Clibborn's Quaker heritage. It had clearly already made an impact on the leadership of the Assemblies of God because that same issue of The Weekly Evangel contained a reference to Quakerism: "The Pentecostal people are uncompromisingly opposed to war, having much the same spirit as the early Quakers, who would rather be shot themselves than that they should shed the blood of their fellow men."

Great Britain banned Blood Against Blood after introducing conscription in 1916, but in 1917 the American Assemblies of God still advertised it in The Weekly Evangel by reproducing fourteen powerful antiwar lines. They quoted such eminent Christians as George Fox, "I cannot fight for the spirit of war is slain within me" and Tertullian, "Our religion teaches us that it is better to be killed than to kill." Arthur Booth-Clibborn inspired many "young conscientious objectors in their personal turmoil, and by his advocacy of an ethic with elements of social radicalism" he challenged the conservatism of established denominations. "I have realized that the more the Salvation Army comes into favour [sic] with the unconverted wealthy, and with statesmen and politicians, the conservatism which this entails makes it very difficult if not impossible for it to preach the whole Gospel."

The Booth-Clibborn family had an impact on early Pentecostalism through the numerous articles printed in The Pentecostal Evangel. Arthur Booth-Clibborn authored thirteen from 1918-1922, while William penned six articles from 1915-1926 and Eric published five before his death in 1924. Theodore, Lucile, and Genevieve each had one article printed.

It is our hope that by making this early twentieth century work available we can encourage both new and renewed commitments to Christian nonviolence and peacemaking similar to that which was evident among so many early Pentecostals. And although our witnesses will necessarily be different than Booth-Clibborn's, for many of us do indeed participate much more in social movements for justice and social change; Booth-Clibborn's deeply Christian arguments for abstaining from violence and killing continue to resonate.

Paul Alexander, PhD

This introduction is a revised excerpt from chapter three of Paul Alexander's,
Peace to War: Shifting Allegiances in the Assemblies of God
(Telford, PA: Cascadia, 2009).

My people are destroyed for lack of knowledge.

Hosea the Prophet

SUMMARY OF THE PREFACE TO THE FIRST EDITION

After labouring for fourteen years in the French and German languages in France and Switzerland, I went to Holland and Belgium and learnt Dutch and Flemish.

The English and the Dutch are the races which first issued the Bible in the language of the people. On the eve of the twentieth century these two races became engaged in mortal conflict in South Africa. They fought in the presence of the heathen to whom they should have been missionaries.

Living at the heart of things, reading reports of that conflict from both sides and in various continental languages, knowing families in both armies, studying also the war from the standpoint of a missionary, I was led to issue this book.

PREFACE TO THE SECOND EDITION
September, 1914

In response to pressing appeals I send forth this second edition with the earnest prayer that the Kingdom of Christ which is "not of this world" may be advanced.

During the past four years I have been engaged in independent Evangelization in various parts of Germany, assisted at times by a daughter and three sons. At this hour many of my personal friends, brethren in Christ belonging to the various nationalities engaged in mortal conflict out yonder, are passing through a time of appalling trial. Some are in the hostile armies. The tide of war has submerged houses and homes where we have met for prayer and soul-saving. Belgian streets and halls along the valleys of the Sambre and the Meuse, German along the Oder and the Vistula, where one was privileged to lift up Christ in company with soldiers of the Cross of various denominations, seem to stand out today in the mind's eye all red with the blood and glowing with the fire of another kind of war—one of a demonic order.

And so I make no apology for the somewhat vehement character of this book. The Christian world which has so long, by its own confession, been playing with vital truth, is now face to face with the most appalling realities.

The awful voice of cannon, the bursting shell and the exploding mine speak with no uncertain sound. It behoves us Christians to be equally direct and uncompromising in the language we use concerning the opposition between the two kinds of war; and all the more because we speak in the Name of the LAMB and seek honestly (however imperfectly) to follow Him "whithersoever He goeth." The fact that this presentment of the truth derives much of its illustrative material from the Anglo-Boer conflict need not be a disadvantage. To get a good comprehensive view of any object it is well not to be too close up. A little distance will ensure a better perspective. In this case, where popular passion (and passion is always blinding) has subsided in the intervening years, men are better able to receive right impressions. A message, of the kind this book seeks to convey, can be readily misconstrued at a time when a fierce war is raging, if it deal with the present scenes.

Men's nerves are unstrung. They easily imagine that those who (as Christ-members) are against all war are merely opposed to some particular war, or to some hostile nation, whereas such appeals deal with human beings as individuals who come into the world alone, must go out of it alone, and stand alone, out there beyond the veil where the throne of Christ is set for His redeemed ones, or where—after the 1,000 years Sabbath—the great white throne is set by God for the judgment of those who rejected His son.

In closing, I would repeat, with a conviction deepened by time, words written in 1907:

> **On this subject—above all others, care should be exercised to avoid everything approaching a harsh or judging spirit, especially seeing that such a wide divergence of honest opinion exists upon it, and that soldiers—some of them regenerate men—sacrifice themselves in war with unsurpassed devotion.**

> **Mortal man can only appeal to his fellow. He is not his judge. He himself is fallible, and by nature sinful.**

This book is therefore no dogmatic declamatory assertion of a personal view, an arrogant *ipse dixit*, it is but an earnest appeal addressed to fellow Christians on the basis of their own faith—a faith by which "a great gulf" is fixed between them and the world. The thought is deferentially submitted to them that when our belief in the Cross and the Blood is carried to its logical legitimate conclusion, the result is inevitable; war is anti-Christian.

A WORD TO THE UNCONVERTED

This book is intended for Christians only, namely, for those born from above. None others can understand its inwardness. "The natural man receiveth not the things of the Spirit of God: for they are foolishness unto him ; neither can he know them, because they are spiritually discerned" (1 Corinthians 2:14).

But if it should be read by some unconverted person I would say to such: Let the scenes of war impress this thought upon you: life is ever offered in Christ to the repentant trusting soul at any time and in any place as *instantaneously* as is death on earth's anti-Christian battlefields. There is but one thing in a time of war which you are not required by the enemy to pay for, and that is for being killed. It is done without money and without price. Death is gratuitous. So also is LIFE on the "battlefield" of the Gospel. All is of grace. Salvation is free, for its price has been fully paid by our Lord in His death for us and in our stead on the bloody field of Calvary.

He is indeed the One who has never yet treated any of His thousand promises as "mere scraps of paper."

You may trust Him fully. Do so.

Blood Against Blood

FOR CHRISTIANS ONLY

Foundation
UNIVERSITY PRESS

Amsterdam | Singapore | Berlin | Portland

Contents

CHAPTER ONE

War Carnel

a madness which the worldlings call wisdom

On a crisp winter's night, during the Franco-German war, the soldiers of a French outpost were gaily playing cards before a roaring fire, in a farmhouse of the Jura Range, when they were suddenly called to arms by the challenge of the sentinel.

A shot rang through the night. In a few seconds all were outside, and, for a moment, the expectant bayonets gleamed here and there among the shadows cast by the moonlight. For a moment more that atmosphere of eternal peace, which seems ever to descend from the quiet stars, reigned over the scene. And now let the tense change that we may see and hear.

With a volley and a shout, the Germans break cover and dash forward. An answering volley of fratricide flashes forth to meet them. A stalwart young Teuton officer, with a blond beard, leads the attack. The man who receives his charge as he reaches the little French line is a solid Alsatian peasant; he also is in the vigor and freshness of youth ; he is simple and, uncultured, with a big warm heart; he is new on the field, and this is the first fighting he has ever seen.

A sword thrust, a parry, a quick lunge, and the French bayonet has passed clean through the broad German chest. Two arms are thrown up, an agonized face, with staring eyes full of unspeakable horror, is turned upward for a moment, as if appealingly towards those quiet stars, while an awful cry rings out above the clamor of the fierce fight raging around: "*O Gott, meine Frau und meine Kinder!*" Then the tall form falls forward while the red blood gushes forth upon the snow.

"O God, my wife and my children!" That cry of supreme agony and anguish has pierced the Frenchman's soul. He has understood it only too well; for the languages of Teuton and Gaul have mingled fraternally in his frontier village for centuries. The innocent group in the distant home seems to rise accusingly before him. The sight of that face convulsed with a last agonized, unselfish thought for the loved ones, the sensation of the steel passing through the vital organs of his fellow-man—through, and out beyond—that cry, that scene, whose accumulated horrors seem lit up as by some hellish flash of livid lightning passing through his brain, have done as deadly a work as his own gleaming weapon—he stands transfixed himself: the young Frenchman has gone stark mad on the spot ! Then he, too, falls to the earth beside his foe, his writhing body, his dethroned and tortured mind, faithfully reproducing, as in one complete representative specimen, the whole of the idealism and realism of those scenes of carnage, which in being physically fratricidal, are morally suicidal. And years afterwards, with wild eyes, he is still reacting in the asylum grounds that fratricidal encounter, repeating the while the fateful words: *"O Gott, meine Frau und meine Kinder! meine Frau und meine Kinder!"* Now there was certainly no method in that madness. But that there was logic, or supreme reasonableness in it, who can deny? Was not that sudden insanity the exact expression of the insaneness of all war? Was not his subsequent condition the true embodiment of its inwardness? War is madness.

Quickly,—before any of the sophisms of modern "Christian" civilization about war being a necessary evil, and killing being lawful and glorious when organized on a sufficiently vast scale and decorated with such names as patriotism and progress;—quickly, before any such questions could be thrashed out in that honest rustic brain, before black could be argued white, the bare horrid truth had acted with the power and precision of an arsenal steam-hammer, the supreme unreasonableness of the whole bloody business had produced such an overwhelming reaction that reason itself collapsed under the shock: and just as man had met man and murdered him on that hill side, so reason had met reason and murdered it in that brain. The deadly blow had rebounded with the precision of the unerring science contained in the words of Christ: "They that take the sword shall perish with the sword." Death had been duplicated!

And thus in another home is another widow, now doubly bereaved. It is scarce a stone's throw from the German homesteads just across the little stream which marks the frontier line between the two peoples, till but a few months previously engaged in agricultural pursuits, and mingling freely in friendly intercourse, but now driven in organized herds into mortal conflict, amid scenes of infernal anger and inhuman brutality, utterly foreign to all their own feelings and desires.

"War is hell," said General Sherman, and on that quiet hillside, beneath the silent starry depths of heaven, upon the pure white snow, under the soft silver light of the moon, hell had indeed been let loose, with all the awful accompaniment of oaths and curses in every variety, in two tongues, bursting as the last expression of their earthly career, from men killing and being killed!

Not in the scene of pride and pleasure as a regiment marches through the streets of one of our towns, with measured tread, to the sound of inspiring music, without one jarring note, while bright flags and accoutrements make all look so gay and hopeful—not there do you find the true picture of war. That is false to the reality. It presents one of the captivating, specious lies with which the Powers of Darkness hide the hideous reality till they have brought their victims too far for retreat. Not in those scenes of "martial glory" is to be found the truth: but in the mangled heaps of dead and dying, or in the padded cell where that poor solitary lunatic was often confined. And what is all Europe at this present hour but a succession of padded cells, in which each nation of human beings calling themselves sane, raises up a padding of forts and fortresses against the "insanity" of the neighboring nations, at the cost of an expenditure which they now themselves declare to be intolerable.

This was the impression which forced itself upon me as I studied a frontier map, when engaged, amid many dangers and difficulties, in salvation war in the region where the above described tragedy was enacted. In war all things are inverted. Many a vice becomes a virtue. Lying and spying is part of the patriotic work for which Christian governments secretly pay great sums of money to individuals of other nations, while ready to shoot individuals of their own nationality for similar services rendered to the "enemy".

The stabbing and shooting which is wrong to the individual in private life, becomes right in international quarrels. Reason must submit to a thousand wrenches, and accept a whole education in false philosophy and specious sophistry before it can accommodate itself to war, its principles, its scenes and associations.

Here, nearly all the laws of social life are suspended, the ties of home violated, the very idea of humanity being one great family is denied, in the obligation laid upon husbands and fathers to slay other husbands and fathers, and thus destroy humanity in its very centre—the home.

The very order of age and youth are inverted: as Herodotus said and John Bright repeated with so much force, "In peace the sons bury their fathers, in war the fathers bury their sons." War is therefore a mass of hideous contradictions, and an outrage upon reason and common sense.

There are no contradictions in true Christianity. War is therefore anti-Christian in all its forms. The testimony of the fathers of the Church was unanimous in this respect, and in Reformation days, Erasmus boldly repeated that testimony, saying, "Christ in disarming Peter, disarmed every soldier." "The weapons of our warfare are not carnal, but spiritual," said Paul, in describing the central principle of the overcoming of evil in the world. The words of Christ "Love your enemies" are absolute.

They embody his description of the spirit animating the children of God on earth, as opposed to that controlling the children of the world. And why? "That ye may be the children of your Father who is in heaven, who maketh His sun to shine upon the evil and on the good, and sendeth rain on the just and on the unjust." And in describing the heathen—the unregenerate,—he said: "If ye love them who love you, what reward have ye, do not even the heathen the same.

The difference then between the heathen and the Christian is an essential difference in spirit and disposition and in the means employed to remedy the evils in the world: to the heathen it is carnal power and worldly war, expressed in hatred and ending in death; to the Christian it is spiritual power and gospel war, expressed in love and ending in life. In the one, man sacrifices his neighbor and sheds blood; in the other, man sacrifices himself and lets his own blood be shed. In the one it is Cain; in the other it is Abel. In the one it is apostolic warfare; in the other it is the warfare of apostates.

War is too positive, too definite a thing to admit of any half ways or half measures: It is either from above or from below. If it is from heaven it must be absolutely heavenly, and nothing hellish in it. If it is from hell, it cannot be regarded as a heavenly obligation upon Christians, upon whom" all true obligations are either of heavenly origin or of no authority whatever.

War cannot be successfully performed without deception and lying in a hundred forms. Protestant nations admit this in the politico-military domain as a necessity, while refusing to admit it in other spheres. They recognise spying and falsehood to be necessary adjuncts of war. They therefore adopt in this respect the principle of the Jesuit that the end justifies the means. This alone classifies war immediately. It forces it back within the pale of the apostate spurious form of Christianity represented in one of its culminating forms by the Church of Rome, whose Pope had, till recently, soldiers and a warship.

One of the signs of the apostasy in the book of Revelation was that the wicked woman arrayed in scarlet—the false bride of Christ,—was seated upon the beast—the beast of carnal force and national power. The power of the gospel message to the world and its authority upon mankind must have therefore been seriously reduced wherever Christian Churches or Associations have sanctioned war. If we were to inquire to what degree this injury has been caused to the gospel by its own advocates, an answer seems to be forthcoming in the case of the first evangelist. Saint Peter, previous to his receiving the baptism of the Holy Ghost. He cut off the ear of the enemy. We may therefore conclude that sword bearing Christianity has only a one-eared audience, and that the power of the gospel is reduced by its advocates by at least one half! That the great command of our Lord to His disciples, on the eve of His sacrifice of Himself for His enemies, "*put up the sword*," should have been given in such circumstances and surroundings is surely conclusive.

War is therefore like Christianity—an absolute system. It admits of no discounting, no attenuation. To acknowledge war to be right in some cases is to give away the whole case, and surrender the very citadel of Christianity. "From whence come wars and fighting," asks James, and he answers "From lusts." "No," say some Christians, "from patriotic duty." But the very word patriotism, as used in war, is anti-Christian, for it denies the brotherhood of man, and therefore denies the fatherhood of God.

Fatherland is a wrong word. An "s" should be added, then it is Father's land—the land of our God and Father. But as every land belongs to God, the whole question is settled at once. Men when fighting for land or life, fight for that which is not their own, but God's; and God does not ask *this* help from them! "War, like worldliness, is therefore theft. And "thou shalt not steal" comes once again into line with "thou shalt not kill."

The war of salvation is the destined service of man in a fallen world, and not the war of destruction.

It is true that we each owe a blood tax to mankind, because of the fallen state of humanity. But it is the tax of the apostle who lays down his life and thus saves it, and not of the apostate who saves his life, and thus loses it in the spiritual sense.

And so, as in all such questions of right and wrong, everything comes finally to a point, and that point is *life*—human life.

"All that a man hath will he give for his life," "Is not the life more than meat," "What shall it profit a man if he gain the whole world and lose his own life."

In every apostolic Christian's earthly existence there may come a moment when he will come face to face with the supreme choice, either to do wrong or to lose his life. If at such an hour he has not been forearmed by a clear view of his vocation, and a decision as to his action, he will be of all men the most unhappy—for if in this life only, and its preservation, we have hope, we are of all men the most miserable. But he who knows by experience the value, the glory of the spiritual life, will not hesitate to sacrifice his body rather than his soul—the temporal rather than the eternal.

Blood Against Blood

"But win not even a worm turn when it is trodden upon?" said
an objector to this Christian doctrine. The answer came, "But the
Maker of the worm did not turn when He was trodden upon. He
gave His life a ransom for His enemies."

This is *the one final test of true Christianity*: the life—the willingness
to sacrifice it as a martyr rather than save it in killing others. It is
not necessary to live, but it is necessary to do right. Better to die
than lie; better to suffer than to sin.

And thus it is that in the Revelation, where we read of the mighty
host of the *overcomers* standing before the throne, we find their
career described in these wonderful and comprehensive words,
beginning at the Blood of Christ shed for their salvation, and
ending after a life of testimony, *in their own Blood* shed in bringing
salvation to others.

"And they overcame him by the blood of the Lamb and the word
of their testimony, and they loved not their lives unto the death;
wherefore rejoice, ye heavens."

Note for the Second Edition

The fact that war denies the brotherhood of man by setting against each other in mortal combat portions of a humanity which was originally one, is but another proof that the brotherhood was completely destroyed in the fall, and no longer exists.

The Bible affirms that it only re-appears through the NEW BIRTH. (John 1:13; 3:3 - 8; Gal. 4:3 - 29; 1 John 5:4; 1 Peter 1:23). It is a feature of the NEW CREATION (2 Corinthians 5. 17; Gal. 6:15). A son alone has brothers, and can say "our Father." (Matthew 6:9, 23: 9. See also John 8:44). Hence I use the word brotherhood as existing exclusively among converted Christians. Such alone can pray "our Father." The disciples' prayer (called the Lord's prayer) , is intended for them alone: "after this manner pray ye." No one else is supposed by Christ to be able to live the Sermon on the Mount.

CHAPTER TWO

War Spiritual

a wisdom which the worldlings call deem madness

I heard the incident related in the previous chapter when engaged in salvation war of the most desperate kind in the same Jura Mountains. Many of the worst characters in the country, on both the French and the Swiss slopes, became converted. They passed from death to life—their very hatred of religion and disbelief in all religious people having led them to attack us with fury, and thus come within reach of the life-giving swordblade of divine love, so to speak. The scenes of the foregoing chapter were exactly inverted. And when we were imprisoned in consequence of the riots caused by our opponents, and were locked up as evil-doers or insane (as we were often called), we then, too, repeated the scenes of the battlefield in those "asylums," having the joy of bringing men to Christ even there. And how often have we not heard a cry of joy, such as this: "O God, my wife and my children!" burst from the lips of some desperate character, when he realized that his sins were washed away in Jesus' blood, that the sword of the Spirit, which is the "Word of God, had pierced his heart and made him die to sin, and that now all would be new in his home through his transformed existence. Before his mind, too, in the first moments of new life, had risen the vision of that fireside. Not far from the spot where the foregoing incident occurred, several of us had to take refuge with some friends in a hay loft, after a day of desperate "fighting," to escape the fury of the mob hunting for us on all sides.

We passed the night there. Beside me on the hay lay a brave convert, six feet four in height, who had been famous in the service of the world, the flesh and the devil, and another won from the domination of the Drink Fiend.

It is thus, and in a thousand other forms, that the apostolic war presents a contrast so absolute to the wars of the world, that there can be no lawful cause of hesitation for the true Christian as to which he should engage in exclusively, and in which he should, if needs be, shed his blood.

The contrast is perfect, even to the respective views entertained by the worldling and the Christian as to the *"madness"* or the *"wisdom"* of these two kinds of war.

Take the following incident: a case of "insaneness" from the opposite sphere:— I summarize here the account written expressly for me by a friend who knew the men in question. "Between the first and second Sikh "Wars there was a great work of God among the soldiers in India, and many became men of peace. Two cases were known to me. The first prayed to the Lord that he might not shoot anyone. The enemy fired first and took his leg off.

"The second was more brave and consequently came off best. (Compare the Gibeonites with Rahab.) This man, after conversion, went at once to the authorities asking permission to resign, saying that he could not take pay when he would not be able to do any work of the kind they required, his conscience forbidding him to kill. They refused his resignation, so he said he would do his drill and keep his arms bright, etc., but that he would not fight.

"When they were advancing against the enemy, the order was given to fire, whereupon instead of adopting any subterfuge, such as not firing (while appearing to volley with the others), or firing high, he simply dropped his musket. Thereupon the Colonel promptly ordered him to the rear as insane (probably fearing the effect of his example upon his comrades). He was 'invalided' home. His passage was paid to England, with train and coach to his own door; whereas had he been simply dismissed upon his first refusal, he would have had to make his way home as best he could. And indeed that was all he had asked for."

Such cases might be multiplied. Personally I owe much spiritually to a faithful Minister of the Society of Friends who, in his younger days, forced into service in the American civil war, refused to bear arms, was treated as demented, and went through several of the fiercest battles, that of Gettysburg among others, with a gun tied to his shoulder, doing all he could meanwhile for the wounded and the dying. He subsequently became a man of God of great power, and it was under his ministry I received the baptism of the Holy Ghost which led me to consecrate my own life to the war of redemption in its most extreme forms.

On the other hand the examples of men going raving mad on the field of battle might also be multiplied. Take the following from the book "*Indiscreet Letters from Pekin*", which has just appeared, describing the siege of the embassies and the subsequent sacking of the city by the European and Japanese troops. Truly extremes meet in the culminating triumphs of the cross and the sword.

"A yet more blood-curdling case is that of a British marine, who has been hopelessly mad for weeks now. He shot and bayonetted a man in the early part of the siege, and the details must have horrified him. They say he first drove his bayonet in right up to the hilt through a soldier's chest, and then, without withdrawing, emptied the whole of the contents of his magazine into his victim, muttering all the time. Now he lies, repeating, hour after hour, 'How it splashes! How it splashes! and at night he cries and shrieks.'"

"It washes, it washes white as snow !" How often have the newly pardoned sinner and his friends sung those words in overwhelming thankfulness, when the blood of Christ has done its mighty work of grace? How often have we not seen desperate sinners, till then fighters against God, "go mad with joy," as the glory of the new life has dawned within them?

And are such men, born again of the gentle spirit of Christ, cleansed by the blood of the *Lamb*, to be herded off to the battlefield to kill like wolves?

One of our converts of the Villette Quarter of Paris, a tall Turco, told us with sobs of the horrors he had perpetrated in war. They were too awful for words. Pillage was legalized; outrage and rape accompanied it as a matter of course; his own hand had assassinated resisting victims; brandy, mixed with gunpowder, was drunk systematically, to give the required degree of madness, savage courage, and fiendish heartlessness.

The Turcos and Zouaves are two classes of French soldiers generally held in reserve for the most desperate charges, which turn some uncertain hour of battle into decisive victory. Their fearless fury is proverbial. And at the present hour, when the Christian host is being admittedly driven back spiritually in so many spheres, should not the most extreme faith and practice of early Christianity be brought into the field; that category which declares all carnal war to be wrong, and creates willingness to lay down life if needs be in the spiritual war?

But its power is only found in Pentecostal baptisms of fire, the exact opposite of the fiery baptisms of war. To the world it all looks like madness,—such other worldliness seems folly. No less than eight times in the opening chapters of his first Epistle to the Corinthians does the Apostle Paul establish this absolute opposition, in such passages as the following—"The wisdom of this world is foolishness with God"; "The natural man receiveth not the things of the Spirit of God: for they are foolishness unto him." No true Christian will deny that these extreme expressions are as applicable to the present period as to the one in which they were written.

It was therefore but natural that madness should have been a culminating charge brought against our Lord and His apostles. Henry Drummond considered it to be the opinion which a fallen and abnormal world must necessarily form concerning the normal life, the Christ life wherever manifested. The reader will find his remarkable words in the appendix to this volume.

CHAPTER THREE

Their Combination

deepest darkness

But must one be so absolute? Can one not combine these two principles, and thus have a Christian soldier whose influence will be beneficial upon his fellow men in modifying the fierceness of their wars, or a Christian nation which will help others to reduce their armaments? Are not our armies just the places where Christians are most needed to help prepare their comrades for death in time of war, and in time of peace to use their influence against the cursing, swearing, drinking and immorality which abound in our naval and military institutions, and which, unfortunately, the barrack life and the battlefield have a tendency to increase? Are not Christians meant to be the salt of the earth?

Cannot Christian nations exercise greater influence than others, to promote by Peace Conferences the adoption of more humane methods in warfare, and to force arbitration upon unwilling governments? And are not large fleets and armies useful to inspire respect, and give greater weight on international tribunals to the nations possessing them?

Such are the arguments most in use at the present day among those who seek to combine the principles of Christianity with those of modern warfare. The extent of their influence at the present hour is shown by the fact that they have actually entered the field of practical politics, and, especially since the Czar's peace proposals of 1897, have occupied an immense amount of the time and attention of statesmen and governments.

In a word, they have become popular. But popular Christianity has ever been rather a suspicious term to the followers of the Crucified.

So let us look into this matter closely, though briefly, before going further. Do such views contain a life-giving truth or a deadly error? Are such alliances of principles, naturally hostile, holy or unholy? Must true Christianity adopt or reject them? On which side is the weight of a really evangelical, namely a personally regenerate, Christianity to be thrown? In a word, and to bring it to a point— what must the man born again of the blood and the Spirit of Christ, by the living Word, redeemed from among men, what must he do?

True Christianity is essentially an individual question, for each must die alone. Strongly organized masses of men can and even must in their final expression work destruction rather than salvation, for they take the place of God to the individual. They have given him a conscience made to order. They number him and make him a mechanical part of a machine which must move automatically to save the Earth Empire they have established. By this system he is a soldier first and a Christian afterwards. He is a patriot above all else. He must hate his fellow men for the love of "God and country." He must be systematically blinded to the good points of the men of the nation he is to kill. He must be taught such facts concerning them as will help him the better to destroy. He must be ignorant to be useful. He must know nothing among men but his country and its isms. And this ignorance of one's fellows across man-made frontiers is the very life of war. "You cannot be English, you are too kind," said a Boer woman warrior dying in a trench, to an English non-combatant Salvationist who gave her a cup of coffee.

Only those who have worked for Christ down among the people in such widely contrasting nationalities as those of the Continent and near to the frontiers, can form a true idea of how the systematic cultivation of this ignorance, and the organized discouraging of any good and kind information about "the hereditary enemy" or rival nationality, is considered a sign of loyalty, and is a talisman to favour. This wilfully blind and narrow spirit is the seed of war.

It selfishly cuts up humanity as a whole in the supposed interests of a part. It is essentially anti-Christian. It places kings and countries between the soul and Christ. Can these wars therefore be reconciled with Christianity? Is "the Christian soldier" a combination of absolutely opposite elements? Or is the term destined, as in the early days, to convey one principle of salvation, of union, of peace, of war through the shedding of *one* Blood? Christ is the Leader and Commander of His people. Note the order of the titles. He leads before He commands. He led the way to Calvary. In being killed on the cross by Earth Empire he showed for all time the true inwardness of the empire principle, and settled the question as to whether "a Christian soldier" means a Christian who kills other men as a soldier in one of the so-called Christian armies, or whether he is just the opposite.

Never was an answer to such a question more vital than at the present hour. It is forced upon us on all hands, especially since 1898, when, under the leader- ship of the Czar, the Powers met at the Hague to see if they could not force peace principles upon each other, or upon those among them who would not submit to the obligation to submit their differences to arbitration.

A change has seemed to come over the face of the world since that day, as if we were approaching some awful crisis.

Therefore the question must be faced: Are these wars both Christian and anti-Christian, both wisdom and madness, both a blessing and a curse, both a kindness and a cruelty, both divine and diabolical? Are they both a supreme good, in being the best means for advancing missionary effort among the heathen, and a supreme evil in spreading civilised sin, pride, vice, avarice, selfishness, in a thousand cultivated forms, and war with countless new types of massacring machinery ?

Surely the answer must be found in the very nature of Christianity itself, and in the very blood which is its fountain head—that of Christ.

The question is more imperative than it seems, for a huge European war may be near, and may be launched upon young Christian men (converted, I mean) before they have been aroused to study the question of what is the will of Christ, their "Leader and Commander," in this matter.! That is the only question which has the least importance. The opinions of men are of no value whatever.

The scenes of the Anglo-Boer war may be upon us again in an even worse form before we have time to think. Up to the time of that war, the evangelical, the missionary, the evangelistic, the salvation forces of England had not been brought so prominently into contact with this question. Never had England shipped such hosts of her sons across the seas to a bloody war.

The cannon of the Republicans had pointed not so long before against their French brethren, the Communists, through the very iron doors and gateway of the building which we afterwards occupied in Northern Paris as a citadel of salvation, amid efforts to blow it up with dynamite on the part of the mob. The passing of its lease from a Mr. Dreyfus was the writer's first use on the Continent, of French acquired there just before the outbreak of the Franco-German war. And as if providentially designed to indicate how little human force or militarism was destined to win Continentals to the knowledge of Christ, the red Salvation flag had been first planted in Paris by the hand of a delicate young girl filled with the Spirit of God. "Not by might nor by power, but by my Spirit, saith the Lord." La Maréchale became on the Continent a name as much associated with the gentle though fearless power of divine grace, and the lonely work of individual persuasion amid imprisonments and exile, as the name had formerly conveyed the exclusive meaning of inflexible militarism and a state-supported form of Christianity.

And then in 1898 by the Czar's efforts to forward the work of the Prince of Peace, and by the South African war which broke out six months afterwards, the question WHICH was the right kind of war, that of salvation or that of destruction, was forced upon us as never before.

In any case they were forced upon the writer by his very position as a S.A. Commissioner in Holland and Belgium at the time of that Peace Conference, and that war which so quickly followed as a commentary thereon. In both cases he felt led by his conscience as a Christian (quite apart from a Quaker training and the example of 250 years of Quaker ancestry) to stand for one red alone and not to attempt to stand for two, for the blood shedding as well as for the blood once shed. When a congratulatory address to the Czar was sent him for signature, he refused to touch the matter in the name of Christ the Prince of Peace. And during the war, when "comrades," and even those who were relatives, were going out on opposite sides to kill each other, he felt compelled to throw all his force into the scale on the side of exclusively Christian peace and Christian war, and to influence young Christians not to go to fight. In this he was sustained by his comrade in arms, with all the powers of a soul having fought from the earliest years in the holy war of salvation.

In South Africa things were brought to a point, as never before in the world's history, as to the true inwardness of "Christian" wars.

Clergymen, theological students, missionaries, evangelists and salvation soldiers took up the gun, the lance, and the sabre, and entered the field on both sides, marching behind quick-firing machine guns and the mightiest engines of destruction the world had ever produced! Let no one think these lines are written in a captious or criticizing spirit. Let no one think they embody disrespect to Victoria the Great, the last years of whose life were, by a woeful coincidence, lit up by the lurid light of that most agonising of all wars.

Let no one fancy I am about to speak disparagingly of any Empire, of any Cardinal, or Archbishop, or any warrior; of any head of a religious organization, or of the least and last of the Christian soldiers who sincerely believed they were doing right to be in the front ranks of those scenes, which even the worldlings called an inferno.

The question is one of life and death, of right and wrong, and is far too solemn to allow any considerations but those of principle to occupy a moment's thought. It is not a matter of persons or policies, it is not a political question or one of sect, party or ism; it is one which towers far above and far beyond all such considerations, it is one which goes right back to the fountain head of our faith, even to Calvary, to Christ, and to the blood of the Covenant. In the question is war *right or wrong for the Christian*, the safety of the very citadel of Christianity itself is involved.

Those men who died out yonder belonged, after all, to no Empire, to no church, to no organization or sect. They belonged to God, to humanity, to each one of us, as we belong to them. And we must serve our generation in serving the interests of truth as they thought they were doing. And above all, every Christian—every converted man—who marched into those battles, belonged in a double sense to every other regenerate Christian in the world, they were their brothers in Christ by the new birth and washing in the blood.

Let us, therefore, as we look at the question in some of its most tragic aspects, lift our minds above the fogs of prejudice or party, of politics or nationality, let us do so as overcomers, whose spiritual stature makes their heads come over the little partitions which separate nations and organizations,—enabling them to examine universal truth in a spirit of universal love, and recognise fellow men everywhere and brethren in those born again.

One point more. Let us bear in mind that every man who died on those fields forsook at once the country or church to which he belonged. A bullet made him do what his comrades would have objected to his doing all along. He deserted, crossed the frontier. He passed into another world. He can no longer be claimed as an Englishman or as a Boer, as an Anglican or as a "Dopper," as a Methodist or a Salvationist. And so I may speak of those who were struck off the rolls of country and congregation by a ^wish of a sabre, a thrust of a lance, or the impact of a hissing bullet. Their spirit has returned to God who gave it. "What says the Spirit of God upon the matter? The body of Christ was given back to His people by the Earth Empire which slew him. What do the dead bodies of these our dear fellow-Christians, precious converted men, say to us? We can ask the question for at least now, they belong to us all. What would their lips say to us if they could speak? Would one of them return from heaven to fight again in that hell? Yet more. Christian war involves a double denial of the central law of both natural and supernatural being—life reproduced by love. The worldling knows only one kind of brotherhood—that in Adam.

The Christian knows two, that in Adam and that in Christ. In war the worldling denies one kind of tie in killing his fellow-creature; the Christian denies two kinds—he kills his fellow-creature and his fellow-Christian. War is thus shown to be at least twice as evil for the Christian as for the worldling. But if we take into

account the incalculable difference between the temporal and the eternal, then the participation in these hatred-breeding, life-destroying, infidel-making scenes of carnage is infinitely worse in the converted than in the unconverted.

Besides, the former has ever a "field" (a battle-field) open to him which the latter has not: he can sacrifice his life as a missionary, and, if needs be, as a martyr, and "sow himself" thus as a seed of righteousness and life-producing life rather than as a seed of sin and death-producing death, which every sacrifice of life on the carnal battlefield inevitably is!

Let us glance for a moment at another kind of devotion to the death shown on those fields. Few wars have witnessed greater self-sacrifice on the field of battle among ministers of all denominations. Their conduct, humanly speaking, was all the more heroic because they had none of the stimulus of the cheer and the charge, and the thought of carrying an instrument of death against those death-dealing instruments in front. They knelt beside the dying while the dreadful duet of Mauser and Lee-Metford hummed and sighed above their heads and past their ears. One Salvation Army officer distinguished himself by a bravery of the Calvary kind as he passed among the wounded and dying, very often himself under fire. He had the privilege of being a soldier of Christ exclusively on those battlefields, not being one of the British troops. But how enviable was his lot compared to that of his comrades who were "soldiers" in both the kinds of fighting, and whose duty it would be at one moment to shoot a Boer, and the next while lying shot by his side, and unable to kill any more Boers, to speak to him about his soul and point him to the blood of Christ. Now that he has no more strength to charge or to kill, his country allows him to spend his last breath religiously, and even to seek to save the enemy beside him! Can anything be more tragic, or sum up in one common-place scene of death of "mothers' sons" on those fields of hellish strife, the evidences of the truth of the doctrine that war is essentially anti-Christian? This view is no complicated science.

The application of common sense suffices. Such contradictions are too glaring, too appalling, to admit of any possible reconciliation between them. So intensely impressed was I at the time by this awful climax of contradictions in this culminating period of the

Christian era, that I wrote the following verses and pinned them upon the wall of my office in Amsterdam. It was like putting down a landmark. The act helped me to define and declare my position. I was at that time receiving strongly worded letters from Dutch people demanding that I should write a prayer for the success of the Boer arms and publish it in our paper. I made it known that I was opposed to all war on Christian grounds. I felt obliged to endeavour, whatever the result might be to me personally, to dissuade Christian men from going out on either side, and was successful.

THE LEADEN LANGUAGE OF WAR "LAWS."

Not till the cannon's roar is hushed,
The Maxim's rattle stilled;
Not till the Christian foe is crushed,
The needed number killed,
Dare any raise a Christian song
Or stop a soul to save;
Would be to death a deadly wrong.
High treason to the grave.

For Christian war to have fair play
The Christ must quit the field ;
For just revenge to win the day
His grace to guns must yield.
No awkward scruples may divert
The gleaming weapon's thrust.
Conscience must no crude claims assert
Where blows must be robust.

The end shall justify the means!
Misgivings stand aside!
A traitor he who intervenes
As we to battle stride!
Let none unnerve the arm that smites.
The heart to pity steeled;
Or dim the eye which down the "sights"
Aims death across the field!
Forward! The record we must break;
Too few are being killed;
A better bag our troops must make.

Blood Against Blood

Our vows must be fulfilled;
We must account for more to-day
Than yesterday were slain:
Forward as Christians to the fray.
And win the fight again.
On! on! ye "death or glory" men;
Sustain the flag's renown;
We must at least lay low our ten
For every one they "down."
Give them the lead of law, my boys:
Your Christian souls be strong!
Our Christian shells shall be no toys;
Christians! avenge the wrong!

Brothers, shall we such words approve.
Their spirit justify.
As true to Christian faith and love
And gospel charity!
But if their honesty appalls,
Their truth be found too true,
How fell the power which men enthralls
Who fight as these men do.

CHAPTER FOUR

The Opposition
brightest light

We have heard of "a light that never shone on land or sea. "There is a light of Truth which has indeed never shone on the land or sea battles of so-called Christian nations. They have *not* had its blessing. And why? It is the light of a full and pure Gospel which only appears when carnal war and spiritual war are placed in absolute opposition, in complete contrast as being the exact antithesis, the one of the other.

Then, and not till then, does the true Light shine forth. And it does so with an effulgence which makes one take in almost every aspect of the question in a moment of time. You *feel* what I mean, though the truth is so great that I am powerless to express it. To do so, one must search nature for a parallel among its final and absolute phenomena.

Let me try. Look at those huge electric lights hung aloft in stations, streets and large shops. Inside them are two thick pencils of carbon, placed exactly opposite each other, with wires leading from them to the opposite poles of a powerful dynamo. To the one pencil is brought a current of positive electricity. In the other the current is negative in nature. When they are placed close together and in opposition, and the current is turned on, then the light flashes forth with dazzling splendor—as the electric "fluid" leaps the space between them. Two negative poles brought together would produce no light—nor two positive either. Nor would the light appear if they were placed too far apart. The power of the light will be in proportion to the strength of the current. The positive electricity always runs from south to north, from the warm life-giving regions towards the cold, bleak regions of death.

So much for the material fact. Now for the spiritual application. With this qualification, however, that no parallel drawn from unfallen nature is ever exactly applicable to the fallen state of our humanity. The normal cannot fully illustrate the abnormal, though our Lord Himself used many such similes, such as those of light and darkness, life and death.

Let us take the negative pole as representing the forces of destruction, the law that sin means death, and that sinners can never correct or improve each other, except by the final process of killing each other, when of course it is too late for the dead to profit by the lesson.

Take the positive pole as representing the gospel of Christ's salvation, which brings life. In order that the light should shine forth there must be two things—opposition and close contact. It was so at Calvary—where the pole of perfect love came into opposition with that of perfect hatred, the false religion of self-righteousness with the true, that of salvation by grace—the Beast life with the Lamb life.

Thenceforth "The Light that never shone on land or sea" flashed out from Calvary with divine effulgence for all who, feeling themselves to be lost, seek for the way of salvation. From the positive to the negative, it beams and blazes. As each act in the dark drama proceeds, a higher voltage, as it were, flashes across our view.

The spear of Caesar and Caiaphas only succeeds in opening a path to a new life through the Saviour's pierced side. The Judean grave only serves to demonstrate the fact of Christ's superior Kingship, as He breaks the Roman seals on His tomb, and the indestructibility of Divine Life, as He rises from the dead. Thus it is that spiritual *light* streams always and only from Calvary, and from the application of Calvary principles, by Calvary love and Calvary life, all down history, even to the humblest act of faith and faithfulness of one of the least of the Lord's brethren. *Nowhere* else is there *any* light for mankind!

As long as Christ had gone about the land in freedom doing good, the light did not shine *in its fullness*—though it had gleamed out wherever the dark negative of sin, disease and death had come in contact with the Holy One, the Healer, the Redeemer; and when cold pharisaical self-righteousness had come into opposition with the warm, forgiving, healing love of Christ.

But at Calvary, Christ is a captive. He is nailed up between two thieves. With the perfection of blindness and miscalculation necessarily characterizing a fallen spirit, Satan himself has fixed the positive pole in position and forced the negative into opposition and contact. There they are: the chief priests, the earth powers, the condemned brigands, and The Christ; and there are the nails and the spear. The one represents earth, fallen man and his systems of salvation, correction and condemnation. The other represents heaven, and the law of self-sacrificing Love and Divine grace. The culminating current of Divine power is turned on between heaven and earth. Light appears. It grows with the growing darkness and the approaching death.

Each word or act of scorn makes it shine the brighter across all space and down all time. The "seven wounds" and the "seven words" of the Cross utter the law of salvation through all history with unmistakable distinctness. Men learn that "by His stripes we are healed." The light streams from the Cross and the open tomb, backward to the gates of Eden and forward to the end of the coming millennium. It lights up Abel's altar and Cain's, it illuminates the Jewish sacrifices of blood, it shines on the history of every martyr who has suffered for spiritual religion as opposed to carnal, for inward faith as opposed to outward force. It shows the meaning of them all.

Apply this to the question of war. *It* is the culmination of all that is negative. Apollyon (of which some have fancied they heard an echo in the name Napoleon) means destroyer. Jesus means Saviour. Place war in its true position, namely, *in exact opposition to Christianity*, let the gospel of salvation be taken as the complete antithesis of men's laws of destruction and then, and not till then.

A Blaze of Light Shines Forth

Attempts, in the least degree, to reconcile Christianity and war, put them even in incomplete opposition, and men cannot see the truth, for there is no light. The period of the deepest darkness in the Middle Ages coincided with that of the Crusades, when the Cross and the Sword were in unholy alliance for the insane work of rescuing an empty tomb and a no longer "holy" land from the domination of the "infidel." Both sides were practically infidels. The "cross," so-called, was but a sword handle; it seemed to wish to force its way to Calvary's mount in order to give the lie to all that Calvary had meant, and plant there a blood-stained "banner of Christ," which was really one of Cain. Two negatives fought for possession of Calvary's hill.

Result: the hour of deepest spiritual darkness of the whole Christian era. Never did bigotry, superstition and lifeless formalism reign so completely in Europe under the name of Christianity, as in the days when it poured forth its life blood, and sent hundreds of thousands of its sons, host upon host (even thirty thousand men, women and children at one time) to die of the sword and the pestilence, in the vain effort to improve the Saracens off the face of the earth, in the name of Christianity! For nearly two hundred years the fury of folly reigned—and that organized madness was called "the holy war".The last king to carry the "banner of the cross" against the infidel at the head of 60,000 Frenchmen was canonized by "the successor of Saint Peter," and became "Saint Louis."

Such is the culminating madness of carnal wisdom. Christ was not in the grave. He was just at that hour teaching lowly Christians in the corners and valleys of Europe to seek Him in the Scriptures. In the depths of the darkness of the Middle Ages, the true light was beginning to shine, and to shine where? Far away from the gorgeous armies, the courts, the thrones and the triple tiara of the Pope, "the King of kings" upon which the word "mystery" was written, till Luther pointed it out (Revelation 17:5).

Mystery, indeed! Egyptian darkness! And the true nature of this "Christianity" was soon to be manifested in a most striking way. When at last the Crusaders were weary of fighting the Saracens, and fought amongst themselves in Palestine, and the scandal became too great for endurance, the hosts were brought back to Europe *and were at once employed to crush the nascent Bible-reading movement which was soon to grow*, through the fires of martyrdom, *into the Reformation!* The sword, till then, fighting as the ally of the "cross" (falsely so-called) on the bloody battle-fields of Palestine, and *wounding* and *killing* there where Christ had gone about *healing*, was now turned against the true disciples of the Cross —repeating once again the scene of Calvary, and placing in juxtaposition the negative and positive principles, till Europe blazed once more with light . . . from the martyr fires! "O holy simplicity!" said Huss, as the poor benighted "Christian" peasant, in loyalty to Rome and in supposed obedience to "Christ," placed a faggot upon his martyr pile—thus hoping to increase his own chances of promotion to Paradise. In Spain, 30,000 "heretics" were burned by the "Christian" inquisition. During three centuries, from 1492 to 1808, thousands of them were slain simply for being lovers of the Scriptures. The last of all to suffer death at its hands (even so late as 1826) was—(striking coincidence!)—a humble and faithful Quaker schoolmaster. Thus God had permitted that the last to seal his faith with his blood in the land where the fires of the Inquisition lingered the longest, was a member of the Society of Friends—that religious denomination which has for 250 years borne a testimony against war in the name of Christianity, against mere brute force as a means to spiritual ends. A death of honour, indeed!

To show the final degree of blindness attained by "Christianity" when it touches the iron tool in anyway, we may recall that Pope Paul IV announced that the Spanish Inquisition was founded by the inspiration of the Holy Ghost. Muzarelli called it "an indispensable substitute to the Church for the original gifts of miracles exercised by the Apostles." In the extreme irresponsible judgments of the tribunals of clerical intolerance, we hear the same metallic ring as in the arbitraments of the sword. Truly, the clashing of swords and the clanking of chains are strange sounds with which to accompany the effort to make men bow to the cross of Christ. But the cross of the Inquisition and the Crusaders only showed a dead Saviour in the name of a dead religion. While seeking on the one hand to rescue an empty grave in Palestine, they endeavoured on the other to destroy in Europe the true followers of the Cross in whom Christ—the risen Christ —lived! The blood and fire of the *auto-da-fé* is the absolute antithesis to the blood of redemption and the fire of Divine Love. Such association would, one would think, *classify* the sword sufficiently for every impartial Christian mind.

But the Jewish wars? some will say. The Jewish wars have not the remotest connection with "Christian" war, as is shown in another chapter. Far from justifying the latter, they condemn it. They were the expression of divine, not human law, in action, and of judgment following sin at once. They belonged exclusively to the Theocracy —divine earthly government—which no longer exists, and they were accompanied by stupendous miracle, earthquake and fire from heaven, which no one claims to be the case in our Gentile wars. They were the expression of eternal laws, like that of gravitation, applied to the moral sphere for a time, to show the connection between sin and death. They destroyed the irreligious Israelite equally with the irreligious Canaanite. And with such divine precision did their retributive force act, that not one stone of the temple was left upon another, when the Jews had forsaken their God and rejected the law of life by faith.

Therefore to attempt to "rescue" that vacant staring temple site from the "unbelievers" by the sword, in the name of Christian "faith" was the culmination of unbelief, the perfect paradox of organized folly.

Fallen man alone, smitten with an utter blindness, could have been capable of such an absolute inversion of the principles of his Christian creed. No creature in the brute creation would have made such a mistake. No animal will feed on ashes. There is no deliberate suicide amongst the dumb creation.

A double commentary was thus afforded by those two hundred years Crusades succeeded by six hundred years of Inquisition by the same hands—upon the attempt to rescue the site of Mount Calvary by restoring a counterfeit imitation of the abolished law of Mount Sinai, and that for the service of the Political Kingdom of the Roman Pontiff—and at the cost of a banished or a burnt New Testament. Thus was demonstrated the true inwardness of the carnal sword when requisitioned to rescue a "holy land" or defend a "holy religion" in the name of a "holy see."

There is something of the madness of the Crusades and of the murderousness of their younger brother, the Inquisition, in every remaining vestige of so-called "Christian" war. It helps to intensify the moral darkness which covers the world.

CHAPTER FIVE

Blood Against Blood

The Cain principle and the Abel principle, the Beast life and Lamb life, War and Calvary, the massacring hosts, and the holy army of martyrs—each utters, at its own culmination, a truth which has been written in red on black all down human history, and which cannot be written on white in grey or in green, whatever the new theologies or theosophies, the new peace systems, or the new social reformations of modern days may say or do.

The descending stream of blood represents that coming from the pierced side of the Saviour on the cross. The transversal stream bursts from a bayonet wound made in the breast of a Christian by a fellow- Christian. They form a cross signifying that Christ is crucified afresh by these so-called Christian wars. They are at right angles to indicate that they represent systems of force, salvation and safety which are mutually excluding and never reconcilable. On the back is the spear of Caesar which made Christians, and the Christian gun and bayonet which make infidels. The first opened in the Saviour's side "the fountain for sin and uncleanness." The second opens for converted Christians a new fountain of hellish war in which they can get back all their sin and uncleanness, with a large addition.

Were a system required to ensure the spiritual blinding and backsliding of simple-minded Christians, and to march them back into deeper sin than that which they had left, none could have been devised more perfectly adapted to the end in view, than that of war, the military system, and official association with the empires of earth and their cruel quarrels. The Anglo-Boer struggle presented one of the most terrible features of war, in circumstances unparalleled for centuries. Family ties, homes, and homesteads were put into the mill of militarism, and ground up as never before in the name of sacred Christian obligations to God and country. Among the Boers the destruction of Mauser-wielding fathers and *mothers*, brothers and *sisters*, and the dying of little children in. Concentration Camps had to go on under each other's very eyes, while among the English the death of loved ones went on at an immense distance. Each opposite extreme of the destruction of home ties was thus reached. And as if to crown the climax, it all occurred in the presence of the heathen, while above the Christian armies engaged in mutual destruction, and as if to give them its blessing, waved the standards of the Christian churches, in two hostile halves.

Christianity is the only remedy to war. Not a bloodless gospel on the one hand, not an adulterated evangelicalism on the other. It must be Blood against blood. All intermediary systems, all efforts to mix these two forces and bloods by either Christian reformers or reformed pagans, have only one effect in the long run, to create martyrs for the truth by adding to the great lie of all time, and thus perpetuating the persecuting spirit in new forms, and the wars of men under new "religious" cloaks.

The remedy for war, and the sin which produces it, must be as extreme, as costly and as painful, as the disease it has to remove. It is the fashion just now to consider the bloodiness of Calvary as too unpleasant a subject for polite ears. Our modern humanitarianism would do away altogether with the doctrine of the cross. The vulgar spitting, the crown of thorns, the mocking enthronement, the seven hours hanging on wounds, the pierced side, are disagreeable subjects. For if they mean anything they mean "the exceeding sinfulness of sin," and the completely "lost" state of the most comfortable moralists around us, apart from personal salvation by the cross of Christ. Many new theologies and theosophies "despise the blood of the covenant." A religion born of the supposed innate goodness of fallen human nature is more pleasing to the drawing-room Christianity of the day, or the self-satisfied sufficiency of Socialism or Caesarism.

The sanguinary gospel is quite too shocking a subject for refined ears, even of modern French Protestant "liberals" (unitarians). They mockingly call it l'evangile sanguinaire. And yet these men of culture are the descendants of the Huguenots who were chased with fire and sword through the Cevennes for their persistence in keeping the Bible open, and the counting of whose carcasses had furnished figures for the great "reckoning" of St. Bartholomew's— the paying in blood for their liberty to believe in the all-sufficiency of Calvary's sacrifice to save the soul, without the "dead works" of ceremony or sacerdotalism. It is an insult to the culture of the twentieth century to suggest that its most exquisite moralists are hopelessly lost unless they "go under the blood" to be saved, just as must the last of Parisian *Apaches* or London *Bill Sykes*, or that on the other hand they must pay for their public quietness in sin, by armed force which finds its culminating expressions now and then in the awful scenes of a march on Pekin, a Spion Kop, or a week of ceaseless carnage, as at Mukden.

The gruesome element must be removed. The howls of agony of the distant battle-field must be drowned by the intervening peals of martial music. Too realistic descriptions of the horrors of a modern "field of honour" "where human beings," "white", "yellow" and "black" are ground together with mules and horses into one indistinguishable heap, by the explosives prepared by a man of science, a deacon in a Christian church, between refreshing cups of tea, in a quiet, peaceful laboratory behind a cosy suburban residence, far away from the deafening crashings of lyddite among masses of human beings—these realities, these contrasts must be put aside when they intrude themselves too gruesomely at the British breakfast-table. The children must not be allowed to look at the photographs of Boer and British corpses lying together in a trench.

For perhaps "Uncle" is there—or perhaps even "Pa." And as to the cross—well, let young ladies decorate it with garlands and lilies at church festivals, and sing of "a green hill far away," between two very modern German love songs, all forgetful of the frightful scenes taking place on the brown hills of far away South Africa, and all ignorant of their direct connection with Calvary, by antithetical opposition. But for pity's sake, don't force disagreeable things upon us: really, our nerves won't stand it!

Do we really realize what our evangelical Christianity teaches? It is extremely "extreme." The truth must be rejected or defended—

not with supineness, but with the utmost energy—for Christless theologies, or reformed religions, which have reformed Christ Himself, are knocking loudly at the door. There is a charge contained in the Book of the London City Temple pastor which has lately appeared that will have to be met. We cannot pass it by. It blocks up the narrow way completely; and it is well that it does so. Evangelical religion ought not to try to pass beyond.

It is the fifteen centuries of awful "Christian" wars for which he holds orthodox Christianity responsible. It has never dared to say war was wrong. On the contrary it has blessed the swords, the banners and the guns!

Christian father! hold up your hands; open them; then get your baby girl to hold up one fat group of five fingers; then get your eldest boy to hold up one finger ; put the fingers all in a row, and count them : there are sixteen. They represent the centuries since "Christians" first began to become soldiers, as a, to them, normal profession. Your boy's forefinger can represent the present century. "Will it one day point on a war map the path by which a position is to be stormed at some awful sacrifice of life, with a Christian "courage" renewed by Japanese example—or will it press a button by which a German Dreadnought and its thousand heroes will "go to glory"? Our evangelical doctrine is too extreme to be easily altered. It levels down genteel and vulgar sins into one black mass. It declares that the most honoured of earth's unregenerate moralists or scientists, the most generous of its millionaire supporters of social work—have equal need of salvation, by the most awful means possible— the bloody cross of Christ, yes, equal need with the most degraded criminals of our slums, wallowing in the back-wash of our selfish civilization.

And at the opposite pole? Will it not *now* at least declare the *equivalent* truth, or else haul down once and for ever the red flag of Calvary? Will it not dare to affirm that the gruesomeness of Christian war has nothing Christian in it? That it arose solely and exclusively with the great apostasy? That the martyr and not he who kills is authentically Christian? That it was only as Calvary became gradually meaningless in practical life that the other red commenced to blot the fair annals of Christian history, hitherto unstained, even though martyr blood underlined every phrase of

Blood Against Blood

witnessing upon its pages? Will they not recognise that the progress of apostasy is clearly defined in history, and has been universally recognized by evangelicals? Let us read into it the language of modern flags and rags—gorgeous war and squalid slums. The flag which Christ first handed His troops when ascending to heaven for a time was *blood red*.

At the close of the first century we see patches of discolouration upon it. Our Lord Himself describes some of them in His messages to the Seven Churches. The process went on, ever larger portions of the flag turned from red to pink, from pink to a dirty white. At last only in corners and along the haft did the glaring red linger. Then came the Roman Emperor Constantine. There had been gradations naturally between, but let us accept him as the typical figure in the great change then about to take place. Paganism and Christianity became fused—or to change the simile, the Lamb lay down beside the Wolf. The result was inevitable.

The process just described became inverted. Gradually "the banner of the cross" began to become red once again, but with a dye of another origin. "Christian war" with the sword began to be looked upon as normal and necessary. The world must be won. Had not Christ said " Go ye into all the world and preach the gospel to every creature"? "Was not the sword a good instrument wherewith to clear the way for the cross ? The other way had been found too narrow, the other gate too straight. "You can't live at that level," people had said. "Such extreme ideas are not practical. And so the progress went on, until at last it issued in the Crusades and their corollary, the Inquisition. The washed-out flag of Calvary had been re-dyed. This time it was with the blood of Cain, not of Christ. And meanwhile in holes and corners, in caves and dens of the earth, a re-opened New Testament was preparing once again the true flag of Calvary, dyed with the blood of the Master, and of those endeavouring with faithful, though faltering footsteps, to follow their crucified King! It was being raised aloft by Albigenses, Waldenses, and Hussite Moravians.

And now, we are once again at an hour of crisis. Peace, peace ! is the cry on all hands. Away with the Christianity which makes these divisions! they cry. We are all one! These good moralists, these Piccadilly roues, are all on the natural upward road. All are equally

33

engaged in a quest after God—unregenerate "millionaires" of money, or of political power, or of human will force—are all one, and can share equally in the social effort of man to save his own world on material lines. Calvary's red flag is meaningless and therefore valueless. So speak the new socialistic forces and theologies.

Can this be all right to us common-place evangelicals? No! To us above all others an inexpressibly awful delusion must lie behind such views. But how are we to make a stand against them? Get back the glaring gruesome complete *red* of Calvary's flag. That is all. Separation! " Come out and be ye separate." Get back to true "Christian war" by getting away from the false. Look at so-called "Christian war." What can be more deluding?

The inexpressibly awful realities of the distant battle-field are hidden from the eyes of English, French and German homes behind the gorgeous uniforms, the splendid music, the proud martial air of carnal superiority borne by masses moving with mathematical precision, accompanied by mighty mowing machines of death, provided by the highest Christian science of destruction. They pass by under gorgeous flags with double crosses upon them. On, on they move to the great harbours where float in their sombre glory the awful Dreadnoughts, and on and on across God's health-giving briny seas, on to the grim, gruesome climax. And meanwhile the officer occupies a superior position in the ball-room, and the highest national honour is heaped upon the returning conqueror. A place is kept for his tomb in St, Paul's or in Westminster Abbey, They have had recourse to worldly arms under a Christian cloak. The highest honours of the world are theirs. Meanwhile the lowly, lonely evangelist may wield his (absurd) sword of the Spirit, the Word of God (forsooth!) in the corners of the city or the world, and preach a Saviour whom the highest culture of the day crucified between two *thieves.*

Earthly empires have always sought to insure their own lives add perpetuation in power at all costs. They are actuated by purely animal or beast instincts. They can know nothing of Calvary. The sword is their natural emblem, for it embodies their *policy* of *insurance.* They must crucify the Christ principle, whose central force is a life insurance of an exactly opposite kind. And what would happen if, in a London Queen's Hall, a Paris Trocadero or an Unter den Linden some extreme preacher of salvation by Blood were to stride across the downward course of our modern Christianity, and say that Christian war with worldly weapons was a ghastly crime against Christ? And if he were to add, as I venture to point out in this book, that the price for which Christ was sold was exactly the price of a modern "Christian" gun, and if to give emphasis to his holy protest, and to show that he was not going in his own name, but was treading upon holy ground, he were to take off the shoes from off his feet. What would happen? You know. He would be called mad of course.

And if he were to go on to say that such an unnatural alliance of opposite principles, carried into the political sphere and expressed by that between Christian England and Pagan Japan for the "peace" of the East was utterly anti-Christian, and a sign of a culmination in our country's apostasy, what would be his lot? You know. He would be called bad of course. He would be " a traitor.

And some would perhaps go to endeavour to get his friends or even his wife or children to say he was both mad and bad and thus doubly secure his moral death warrant.

Such action would be probably out of time and out of place. We are no longer in an outward dispensation such as the Jewish when symbolic action was a suitable form of preaching and was understood by all. But we have only to imagine the case to obtain a true picture of the reception such witnessing would meet with.

History, carnal and spiritual, *always does* repeat itself. There thus come hours when "charity," "breadth of view," "Christian submission," "love of peace," are terms which can easily hide culpable supineness and disloyalty to Christ and the red flag of Calvary.

But oh! shall we not arise as never before in the holy revolt of true love, church of the *Crucified* and *only Redeemer*? Shall we not—reversing the old salutation of the Roman soldiers as they passed before Caesar, on their way to war or gladiatorial struggles, *Ave Caesar! Morituri te salutant!* "Hail Caesar ! they who are going to die salute thee"; shall we not passing before the cross cry the same to our King—even at this hour crucified afresh in all the great capitals of earth and their empires? This is no mere figure of speech. Whoever is faithful in this age to all that Calvary means will surely meet with Calvary treatment. The form of crucifixion may differ; but the spirit will be the same. But shall we not be willing thus to help "in our own bodies on the tree—on some modern pillory of disdain—to complete the holy cycle of revelation? Earthly empires dread the red flag of revolution. Let none of us dread the red flag of Redemption. Under it alone is safety.

CHAPTER SIX

Weep Not For Me

During the Anglo-Boer war everyone—"friend" and "foe" alike—was struck by the heroic figure of De Wet. The word signifies the law in Dutch. The name and the man were typical of what Sir Conan Doyle, in his "Great Boer War," calls "a dour, fatalistic religion," and to the hard mechanical effect of which upon the Boers he attributes much of the origin of that cruel struggle. Thus the name "General The Law," at the head of an army of Christian Boers, fittingly expressed the effort to combine two dispensations entirely different, that of the law and that of the Gospel, on the modern battle-field of Gentile nations. In the lonely guerilla, in De Wet the uncatchable but onmipresent, there was a figure of daring and perseverance amidst outward danger, distress, and defeat, worthy of the highest type of gospel soldierhood.

Have not many of us been struck by the self-conscious look of martyrdom, the sort of "weep for me" expression, in the face of our Lord as represented by artists; instead of the expression of calm might, of quiet majesty, and self-forgetfulness which must have been His, and more than ever as He approached the cross. "Weep not for me," was His cry as He staggered up Calvary's cruel hill to the place of a skull. Desiring to have a more probably just "head of our Lord" for a book on war I was then preparing, I sought out a celebrated Dutch artist in his studio on a fourth story in Amsterdam. He placed an easel and prepared to make a rough outline under my direction. It was difficult work, the old lines of the Christianity of the Middle Ages would come back. It was the bad rut. After three visits the head was finished. The expression of calm, triumphant, loving determination was not quite what I wanted, but I give the result in the frontispiece.

Judge of my horror as a Quaker-Salvationist on seeing very soon afterwards in the weekly paper to which this artist furnished the political cartoon, with the masterly touch which has made him celebrated throughout Holland, and which has been repeatedly reproduced in the London *Review of Reviews*: judge of my "seizure" when I saw my "Christ's head" on the shoulders of his De Wet in a trinity of Boer leaders! Under the slouched hat he had produced it to perfection :expression, nose, beard and all. De Wet was his hero, his Christ. "The law" had again found an erroneous modern interpretation in harmony with the Christian gun.

I had a suspicion that the artist has had a subtle delight in this use (minus the cross) of the "head" we had toiled over together. He was a Dutchman and an agnostic; I was an Englishman and a Christian, but not a fighting one. (And yet—yes, but at the antipodes of principle and spirit.)

His action was but another illustration of the effort which has continued up to the present day to force Christianity back to association with destructive weapons, in spite of all spiritual Christians can do to turn it towards its primitive course.

Nothing is more striking than the modern view of the right sort of a face for warriors. The French have an ideal military head—*une helle tete militaire.* It has to be sharp, angular, with an imperious, inflexible, rather hard look, generally set off by a bristling moustache. It must have cold steel in each feature. It must speak of "law": the law of man who kills his fellow man for his "lawlessness"—and gives a wide berth to the true gospel in all its forms.

Blood Against Blood

Notes for the Second Edition

A brother in Christ has convinced me that it is not according to the divine mind for the born-again to take part in making or issuing pictures of our Lord. One cannot find any authorisation for it in the Scripture, but much that tends in the opposite direction. Such portraits must all be a work of imagination and not of reality. They deal with Him whose personality must be infinitely sacred to us. They represent His form under a thousand contradictory aspects. Therefore entire abstention from them seems in conformity with the straitness of the gate and the narrowness of the way.

"Art" has done much harm in this and other spheres, especially through the great Papal apostasy. It has helped people to live in religious sentimentalism and illusion "in the chambers of their imagery"— Ezekiel 8:12. Realities, ghastly in the fleshly sphere, and glorious in the spiritual, are crowding upon us. At this hour the graven images of the apostles and prophets are tumbling from the Cathedrals on the Continent under the fire of "Christian" shells, and the smoke of the ruins of the great Jesuit libraries in Louvain, Malines and Eheims is ascending up to heaven. These scenes are realities which may be pictorial of God's disapproval of the graven image-making (intellectual and spiritual as well as material) which marks all apostasies and the idolatries which characterise them. The same Rome which brought in the images thrust out the Bible. The more we learn to rest our faith upon the word of God alone (according to Romans 10:17), the less will we require "aids" of the artistic kind.

I had intended to leave this chapter out, but found this would alter the stereotyped paging. This circumstance—possibly providential—seems therefore to call for this note and the admission It embodies.

CHAPTER SEVEN

Every True Christian A Seer

There is something of the seer in every new convert to spiritual Christianity. His "eyes have been opened" by supernatural power. He sees as never before. He lives in a new world, unknown to men of this world. If he resist the influences of the half apostate Christianity around him, he will go on seeing ever more clearly, and the gulf between him and it will grow ever wider. He is inspired and impelled by a spiritual life of which it knows little or nothing.

One of the first impulses of every new convert is to look upon war as wrong, and as contrary to the newly born spirit of love and saving mercy within him. To get to believe the contrary he has to be educated in the false philosophy of a low-level Christianity ; his moral nature has to submit to many contortions in the transition. It is something like the process by which a goodly farm lad is turned into a good clown. If the young convert resists and opposes his childlike views to those of his elders, he will be treated as impertinent, on the "who are you" principle: "Dost thou teach us?" He will be shown that carnal war is "a necessary evil," which combats and destroys greater evils.

At last he is, perhaps, persuaded to believe that "some wars are right," especially those of his own country. And thus the whole case is given away. Other powers are teaching him, meanwhile, that his enthusiasm, his first love, is excitement or fanaticism, and if he attempts to evangelise his fellows he will be shown that this is a usurpation of the religious status of his superiors.

He may kill as a common soldier of Empire, but he may not save as a common soldier of Jesus Christ. In that direction, too, he has to be taught, and "his views have to be corrected." It was not so long since lay preaching was abhorrent to the State clergy. It was even so to "Wesley in the early years of Methodism, incredible as that may now seem. For a simple layman to affirm all war to be wrong, while the Established churches of even Protestant Lands and many dissenting sects declare it to be admissible would seem, therefore, presumptuous.

The early Christians *felt* war to be wrong, and new converts do the same to-day. Not till they have been systematically misled and deceived by the semi-pagan sophistries which pass for Christian wisdom all around, not till then do they even begin to reconcile war with the gospel.

But on the other hand, all anti-militarism, which does not grow as a natural fruit on the tree of the New Life, is something artificial, which will produce more harm than good.

Not long ago in Holland, a young Unitarian, son of Calvinistic parents, refused to bear arms when forced by conscription to enter the barrack doors. His refusal was based upon Tolstoyism, a creed which, while denying the divinity of our Lord, and the fact of the resurrection, sees in the Sermon on the Mount the normal means of arresting the progress of evil in the world—non-resistance. It is a purely negative force.

The case made a great stir in Holland. Naturally, the social-anarchist party took it up on political grounds. The Colonel of the regiment sent for the "orthodox" (evangelical) clergy of the State religion, that they might bring the young man to his senses, and prove to him that not only military service and war were not wrong, but that they were a Christian duty, which it was a sin to refuse to perform. A room in the barracks was turned into a theological lecture hall, where, in succession, four pastors, representing different shades of Protestantism, dealt with this one student, to teach him his Christian duty to kill! They poured endless argument upon him, Bible in hand. They did not succeed. The young man would persist in keeping the Sermon on the Mount open under their eyes, and in quoting passage after passage from the New Testament. Deeply chagrined and vexed they left him. He was imprisoned. I went to the central station at Amsterdam to have a word with him the day he was taken through under an armed escort.

But I did not succeed. My object was that he should have some encouragement to continue on the good way and pass on into spiritual life from intellectual truth by personal conversion, but he was kept isolated as much as possible from such influences; besides, such work was not considered part of my official gospel duties in the position I then occupied. And worst of all, a political party was seeking to harness his case to it's chariot. This is one of the results of Unitarian Tolstoyism of the New Theology type. It eventually becomes turned into political channels; it cannot remain on a non-worldly Christian ground, seeing that it is itself a form of worldly wisdom, not being based on spiritual transformation, and on "redemption through the blood. "This is but another proof of the fact that the simple Gospel of the Blood is the only force which can be of any use on the Continent of Europe, for it alone can keep clear of party politics. It is the enemy of none, being the friend of all men. But that is why no political party, as such, can ever be its friend. None care for "the shame of the cross," which is its glory.

The French Anarchist, Sebastien Faure (recently expelled from Geneva) sought to make political capital out of that young man's case in Amsterdam. I heard him base upon it a powerful anarchist appeal in the People's Palace of that city. He was succeeded, on the same lines, by a Dutch Pastor of the freethinking school, which is similar to that of the New Theology in England. His "Christian" anti-militarism was of the social-democratic shade, and of a collectivist category, somewhat like French Herveism. Such is the final goal of "Christian" truths when stolen from their normal setting, and separated from their context! Truth which has not its source in Life, in regeneration, in personal, spiritual conversion, is mere intellectualism, and ends by sitting in the seat of the scornful. The polite scorn with which these modern schools treat the old gospel of the Blood is characteristic of their whole system. It is negative and destructive, not positive and constructive in the spiritual sphere. It merely goes to build up another "thou shalt not." It produces no true spiritual life.

Like their modern parent Tolstoyism, these systems end in some mere negation such as "thou shalt not let any servant work for thee, because there should be no servants. "Thou shalt not let others make thy boots or clean them. All men are equal." And

43

so Count Tolstoy patiently makes his own boots. Such artificial, abnormal, lifeless theories deprive of work servants who would be glad to perform it! They make a non-natural, non-Christian equality. It is the principle of the Versailles gardener who clips rows of the box trees on the terrace of the Palace into one pattern, allowing none of the inequalities of nature to remain. The unregenerate "Liberty," "Equality," "Fraternity" of the French national motto is merely another expression of force. It had to be forced on men by the revolution. Humanity had to be clipped down to one dead level. There must be equality!—and so the "heads" came off. Marat said, "Give me three hundred thousand heads and I will bring in the new era." And the orgie proceeded. But guillotining humanity does not save it. The death and resurrection of Christ, our now living Head, can alone do that; His blood alone is the fountain head of personal salvation, as His ever-living Spirit is the exclusive source of salvation work for others. Beside Danton in the beginning of that Revolution stands the figure of Camille Desmoulins—a gentle, loving theorist, a kind of "new theology" writer for the Revolution. He stood on a chair in the Palais Royal Gardens, plucked an innocent green leaf, and told the crowd to do the same, adopting it as the symbol of the new movement. The leaf period did not last long: the blood-red fruit soon appeared—the Reign of Terror. Nothing could be more heroic than the self-sacrifice of all the parties concerned to their revolutionary theories.

The Girondins' banquet the night before their execution at the hands of a more radical party, coming up beneath theirs to behead all above it, was sublime in its heroic scorn of death.

Their song has become immortal . . .

"Mourir pour la patrie,
C'est le sort le plus beau, Le plus digne d'envie!"

Yes, "to die for the country" (after having killed others) at the hands of those who will be killed in their turn by a lower stratum still, while the successive slices off the top of the social pyramid become ever wider as they descend; this! this is "the most glorious, the most enviable lot" which humanity has ever proposed or been able to propose for itself ! And the result Is there one whit less sin in the Paris of today, or in the Republic of the hour, than in that of 1789? Killing Frenchmen never cured France. Nor did the killing of Europeans cure Europe under the regime of the military dictatorship which succeeded that of the red Republic. These systems belong essentially to "the destroyer," Apollyon. Napoleon would have gone on till, by the killing of a world, he would have cured it. It was a policy of sin its own remedy, death dying by its own sting, the grave being destroyed by its own victory. It was the policy of the tomb in the rock.

Napoleon found his political tomb on the solitary rock of St. Helena. His own principle had worked out its final logic to its conclusion. Christ rose from His tomb, but not so Napoleon, and the extraordinary success of Christ was always a matter of amazement to that Emperor. His words on the subject are probably too well known to bear repetition here. He saw a success which he was spiritually too blind to understand.

Yes, the simple-hearted Christian convert instinctively sees war to be wrong by the *sight* he has had of Calvary, and feels it to be wrong because the steel tool and the cold, clammy hand of death do not strike him as being his natural fellow-workers, in spreading over earth that life-giving gospel which is the only force in which he has really any more interest.

All else is to him but a means to serve that lifegiving work, just as all things else seemed to Napoleon but necessarily subservient to his end of personal universal dominion "for the good of mankind." Thus the object of this book is to help keep the newly converted from being perverted. Standing recently with two of my boys at the huge entrance gates to Napoleon's magnificent tomb in Paris,— gates made of the cannon captured at Austerlitz, I was struck by the last testamentary words of the great warrior, inscribed above the grim portals:—"I desire that my ashes shall repose on the banks of the Seine, in the midst of the French people I have so loved."

I drew the attention of my boys to the parallel and contrast, which I then noticed for the first time:—Napoleon so loved France, that he took millions of her sons, and made them believe on him so utterly that whosoever among them followed him to death might spread an endless amount of death through Europe; whereas "God so

45

loved the world that He gave His only begotten Son that whosoever believeth on Him should not perish, but have everlasting life.— (John 3:16.) Napoleon's wars cost eleven million lives, of which two million were of his own subjects.

Those two boys were born, the one in Paris, Napoleon's capital, the other on a hillside over-looking the Ehone Valley, which Napoleon had traversed at the head of an immense army to force from Nature a passage over the St. Bernard. They commenced life in surroundings of gospel work in both countries and close to "posts" of a war the opposite of his; but being so born, on the soil of these conscription lands, they would possibly have later on to serve in two different European armies, unless they stood in their turn by the cross of Christ in refusing to bear the sword as true soldiers of their Master.

The last time I had stood at that spot was with my own father—a Quaker—when in 1868 he was taking me to school in Switzerland. The day previous we had seen Napoleon III, accompanied by his only son, a boy of my own age, and the Empress Eugenie, pass in state between dense masses of frantically cheering humanity in the Champs Elysees. He was then at the height of his power; it was his birthday parade and review: all Paris was *en fête*. It was also the national holiday of the Assumption, created by the churches which had first allied the Cross to the sword, and the exclusively Roman Catholic and Greek Church doctrine of the miraculous bodily ascent into Heaven of the Virgin Mary.

Little did we think that Napoleon and his family were to have but one more such triumphant day, and that then was to come the catastrophe of 1870, resulting finally in its far off consequences in the death of the young Prince, the hope of the Napoleonic race, at the hands of the Zulus in the wilds of South Africa.

When pointing out to my boys these coincidences—that *Napoleon so loved* and that *God so loved*, and the extension of these two opposing principles through the history of Christianity, I spoke in German out of consideration for the feelings of the old French soldier, an invalid, who was on guard at the tomb. But suddenly he said, "I understand all you say: I am an Alsatian." He came from that frontier land of the two peoples, where the two languages are spoken,—the land over which have poured, in ebb and flow, the fiercest tides of battle.

(Frontier races are always the most exposed. The same is true in spiritual things. The men of the border or of the far-flung outpost, have always to bear the brunt of battle.) The old man seemed very intelligent, and at once agreed with the view that war was not Christian whatever else it was. He appeared much interested as I told him of the "God so loved" before that tomb, the most magnificent of any of the world's warriors, and above which rises an immense cross bearing in life size a dead Christ.

The aged guardian of the dead monarch's dust was wearing one of the sabres used at "Waterloo, a precious relic from the shrine of the idol of Imperialism.

Behind us, in the church, were hung, all round the walls, the tattered blood-stained flags captured from the enemy. They were destined to give martial inspiration to the worshippers, a practice which exists in our Saint Paul's in London, in other forms. The third Napoleon, to add to the glory of his reign and his race, had given the first Emperor the most magnificent funeral of all history, after bringing his body from St. Helena. And France still loves and abhors the memory of Napoleon in alternate bursts of feeling, for although he sacrificed such multitudes of her sons, and reduced the average height of the Frenchman by three- quarters of an inch, he brought her a "glory" she has never had before or since. Napoleon "so loved" France !

Further back behind us in the great Museum of the "Invalids" were halls full of the armour of the Crusaders. It was of all conceivable shapes and varieties, some of it dented by the blows of battle. And above all, hanging from the lofty ceiling, were innumerable "banners of the Cross" used against the Moslem hosts. Some of the complete suits of steel armour were for boys of six or eight years of age. Others would just have fitted my two sons.

And thus generation after generation hands on the lie as it is in Cain, or the truth as it is in Christ, the false "glory" of empire and the sword, or the true glory of the cross and of Pentecost ; and each profits by all the accumulated lessons of its brief presence upon the stage of human life, to extend its own principle into the next generation at an ever higher degree of carnal or spiritual power.

Let us rest assured that God will claim a higher service of the cross from his seers of the rising generation than from all the preceding ones. Why should not every newly converted Christian be kept from the horrors of the past fifteen centuries, by being told from the first hour of his first love, that the first Christians refused to bear arms and were right in so doing.

This result can never be attained by studying any human standards of right and wrong, but by a careful painstaking study of the Scriptures. There we find "the mind of Christ."

CHAPTER EIGHT

Abnormal Light From Below

On entering a theatre to lease it for meetings the proprietor turned up the footlights for me and went on the stage. But we did not require foot lights for salvation work. They give the face even of a Christian an abnormal look, for God has placed man's eyebrows above his eyes and not beneath. And when the light glares upwards on the artificial mask-like faces, powdered and painted, of the artificial world of the theatre, the effect is almost ghastly.

But there are times when men are almost unwilling to receive any light upon the subject of war, except that of the lurid glow which comes from the battlefield; from beneath, from the burning villages, the bursting bombs, and the reddened ground, instead of from above, from God's own gospel Sun in the heavens. Hence the verses which close Chapter 3 and the painful thoughts which force themselves upon the pages of this one. Shortly after penning those verses I received a telegram from the Hague informing me that the news had come to the Boer Committee there that the brother of one of our dear Christian friends had been killed. She was an orphan and he was her only brother. He was the last man destroyed by a British shell beside the Long Tom which had bombarded Ladysmith. I sent for her to my house and shall never forget the scene, while I endeavoured to break the news to her. And it was but one of many. If a Christian is to feel at all on the question of war he must feel strongly. And how can he express himself less strongly and be true?

The Quaker Poet Whittier has said:

> *"For thyself, while wrong and sorrow, Make to thee their strong appeal, Coward wert thou not to utter What the heart must feel."*

Let us examine one of the most striking modern illustrations of the intensified horror and contradiction involved in Christian war. Providence seems to have permitted its preparation—ready to our hand at this precise period of Christian history. And it would not be true faithfulness to the cause advocated here to abstain from adducing it out of personal feelings of human love to the Christian brethren in question, if divine love to universal truth require it. The lives of our brothers on some future battle-field may be at stake.

Let us open the book: "The Salvation Army at work in the Boer War." It is by a lady Adjutant, the daughter of an officer in the British army.

In its upper portion this Salvation Army book bears the royal arms of England, with the rampant lion and unicorn, and the threatening motto, in antiquated French, "evil be to him who evil thinks of it." Below is the Salvation Army crest with its cross, its crown, its traversing swords, its S. of salvation, and the all embracing motto "blood and fire," the blood of Christ and the divine fire of redeeming love.

On page 60 we find the members' pass of The Naval and Military League of the Salvation Army. Its motto is "Love shall conquer." The leaguer's declaration, when becoming a member, after having been sworn in as a Salvation Army soldier, is:—

> *Having the assurance that God for Christ's sake has pardoned all my sins, I am determined to love Him with all my heart, to love my neighbor as myself, and to serve God as a true soldier in the ranks of the Salvation Army. By the grace of God I promise (1) total abstinence, (2) purity, (3) to discourage gambling, (l)to read daily from God's word, (5) to do my level best to bring my comrades to Christ. (Signature)*

Thus the two last names on the card are "Christ" and this Christian soldier's own.

There is no promise to obey the command: "thou shalt not kill." To refuse to shoot would make him liable according to military law in time of war to be court-martialed and to be shot in cold blood by men of his own regiment and even by Salvationist comrades. To "bring comrades to Christ" as a King who forbids war would be to "sow disaffection and disloyalty among the troops." To "love his neighbor as himself" is to kill him more quickly than that neighbor can kill, for that is the culmination of "a good day's work." And yet the word "neighbor" as Christ used it in Luke 10., signified men of another nation rather than men of the same neighbourhood. The Salvationists on both sides were bound by their very position to kill each other. Spiritual brotherhood presented no more obstacle to mutual destruction than does natural brotherhood. South African brothers of the same family serving in the opposite armies were also bound by solemn oath to slay each other.

No one would consider such a state of things abnormal amongst savages, and yet it is just there its official form does not exist, for no savage serves a hostile tribe as a systematic piece of duty. The mere circumstance of having lived in some other part of the Colony, and having had one's sympathies enlisted on one particular side, divided some brothers in those Boer families from the rest, and doubtless if one of them, long before the outbreak, recognizing a seed of future evils in the systematized departure from God's word involved in the breaking up of a home by an earthly organization, in making it subservient to the interests of the army and the country, and had he refused to bear arms, then he would have been looked upon as a fanatic and treated accordingly.

All his acts and words would have been misunderstood and consequently misrepresented, till finally he would have been unjustly accused of being a traitor or a coward.

Such was the lot reserved for the Boers even more than for the English, the family and tribal feeling having narrow geographical limits among the former. And so brothers in grace, and brothers in nature were equally under solemn obligation to shoot each other down.

But "Thou shalt not kill, thou shalt not steal, thou shalt not commit adultery, thou shalt not lie," are all one at the root. The first, second and fourth of these commandments are systematically broken in war. Then why should the third be kept? "Why should men who are taught that to destroy their fellows is right, and that spying and lying and pillage are righteous, feel themselves bound by the middle commandment concerning adultery, the law enjoining respect of the marriage bond which protects the home? The breach of the other three destroys it, no less than would the breach of this. Wherever earthly armies assume the control over human beings, and treat the husband as belonging to them apart from the wife and children, and in order to increase their power and cohesion, set aside the laws of God, then the systematizing of evils in many forms follows as a natural consequence.

A Napoleon can divorce a faithful Josephine simply because she is childless. He requires children to succeed and sustain him in his power, his selfish conquest and his glory. What mattered it then that his act was practically that of adultery? Did he not organise killing and stealing? Why stop there? And was it not he who first organized licentiousness as a necessary corollary to the barracks, in establishing in Europe the hateful police des moeurs, and the "state regulated vice " which Christian England has adopted in connection with her armies as "a necessary evil," to her eternal shame ? When war is considered a necessary evil, then so also are its adjuncts. Thus we see that Christian war is all of a piece with many crimes.

But it has the blessing of the state Christianity, as Napoleon's re-marriage had the blessing of Rome. And yet he did not reach that goal till he had first broken engagements with princesses of two empires, considering they were not politically advantageous enough. Whoever, therefore, as a Christian, takes his stand by the Word of God, and opposes, at their very root and beginning, any organized violation of God's Word in the supposed interest of armies or countries, must expect to suffer in equal proportion at their hand. If he thus obviates crime and assassination he will be morally assassinated.

Calvary shows us that the world renders us just as much evil as we render it good. The proportion remains the same in every true Christian's life. And if he, by training or circumstance, has more foresight than some others, and knows from God's word that certain roots must bear certain fruits eventually, then his foresight will be his greatest offence in the eyes of the men of Earth Empire. Should he, even in their own true interests, and in order to serve them on the highest plane possible, oppose their follies in the name of the "Word of God, he will be treated as a madman in exact proportion to his heavenly wisdom.

When he refuses to adopt carnal methods, or when he resists systematized sinning by disobedience to his rulers, he will be accused of breaking the gospel law of non-resistance, like the boy whom his father struck and killed for attempting to explain why he would not touch intoxicating drink like his deluded parent. The poor lad desired to prove that he disobeyed, not from uppishness or indiscipline, but in love to both his earthly and his heavenly Father. He paid the penalty of his honesty with his life. No greater calamity can befall any sincere conscientious Christian than to be placed under two contradictory sets of laws at the same time, the one normal and the other abnormal, the one divine, and the other of man's invention with merely national ends. But such circumstances have made a Luther before this in another sphere, and a Luther has meant a re-opened Bible. Unspeakable crosses and sorrows may mark the way, but it leads to life and light and liberty divine.

Should any young Christian read this who is thus bound by human "laws," made in open defiance of God's Law, let him remember how small, how trifling in the sight of God are the Empires of this world. Let him remember that he belongs to the innumerable company of the redeemed, of which the immense majority are invisible, but encompass him about as a great cloud of witnesses. Let him remember that he is not merely a child of time, but a child of eternity. Let him set divine Law above human destroying decrees. Let him treat them as cobwebs, and refuse, regardless of consequences, to touch carnal weapons. And no man will ever be really a law-breaker who puts divine Law above all else.

A solitary man of God wrote:—

> "No home on earth have I, No nation owns my soul;
> My dwelling place is the Most High, I'm under His control."

Men's war laws tear Christ's robe in pieces, and break again the body of our Lord. They make men of other nations appear to be " enemies" and oblige those who refuse to bear arms against them, to be considered as traitors or deserters.

Thus the Christ of Calvary, and not the Caesars of earth's thrones, must be the leader and commander of God's people in this question of war as in all other vital matters.

Let carnal wisdom and carnal war but have your finger, and it will not stop till it has the whole body. Let the dogs of war loose and nothing but bones will soon be left. War cannot be Christianized any more than lying or licentiousness. How gladly would the Christian nations of Spain and England, and the allied forces at the siege of Pekin, have stopped short of the culminating scenes of carnage and pillage.

How Christian men shuddered at the Pekin outrages, the concentration camps of Cuba and South Africa, the guerilla war methods of the Boer generals, and the wholesale burning of Boer farms by British commanders. But you cannot stop in war. Death and devastation are its normal goal, and you must go on, on, on to the bitter end, to the last smoking ruins of homesteads, and the last charred remains of fathers, on, on to the last grim, cruel climax. What made those scenes all the more painful was the fact that Christian gentlemen, received in the highest society of all the nations concerned, Protestant generals and statesmen, equally with Catholic, had to direct those final grindings-up by the machinery of war. War is like other sins, give it an inch, and it takes an ell.

In connection with the evangelistic work carried on among the soldiers by Chaplains and others during the war some men are reported as having found Christ only a night or two before they were to die in battle. Meetings were held by Christian soldiers of the Queen, men who preferred infinitely to spend those hours, possibly their last, in such blessed work, rather than in football or in card-playing as did many of their fellows. But how doubly sad that made one side of the question. To bring men to the blood of Christ one day, and cheer them on in a savage charge to shed the blood of fellow-men and fellow-Christians the next day ! What term can qualify such a state of affairs ?

No word will fit the case. Words are either too strong or too weak, because the men were sincere. Therefore we must go back to Calvary for the silent language of the pierced hands and feet. The leaders of Christianity to-day justify war for the Christian when commanded by an earthly sovereign. Nor is it to be wondered at, seeing that nine-tenths of the influence of the older Christianity, especially that of the State Churches, Protestant, Roman and Greek, are on that side, and train up the young in those ideas, that, when some become converted, even in a movement like the Salvation Army, they bring those views with them. In the case of many the military system of this organization keeps it alive, in those who have not enough light to see the difference, much less the absolute opposition between the war of salvation and the wars of destruction.

If the Christian Church were to come out boldly on this question it would meet with much persecution. Its people, to endure these fresh fires with faith and constancy, would have to receive a teaching and training in the Scriptures which they have not now, concerning the difference between the old and the new covenants, and the full meaning of the "blood of the *Lamb*."

Chaplains and missionaries of the armies who went missioning among the soldiers, British and Boer, would possibly not have received passes had they been known to preach that war was wrong, and so, taking into account the position made for them by Christendom as a whole, one must be thankful they got there at all, and were able to do the good they did. This, however, is but another reason why we should draw the highest instruction from the whole situation. They would not save men from war, so they sought to save them in war. This may also explain how it was possible that a climax so startling could be reached as that presented by a "religious department" in modern warfare, where prominent Christians have to be utterly silent upon one half of the gospel of Christ (the social and political side, "put up thy sword") at the precise moment when the anti-Christian gospel of cannon is thundering its loudest! And so as in all such cases our gladness at the salvation of one soul is naturally as great as are the special and awful obstacles of the whole anomalous position.

The Christian soldier is obliged to set the orders of his general above those of Christ in His sermon on the Mount, and to love his own life so much more than that of his fellow Christian in the hostile host that he must shoot him. If, in a spirit of love or self-sacrifice, he allowed himself to be shot and crippled in battle rather than shoot his "comrade" enemy, he would break his vow of loyalty to his king in keeping that of loyalty to Christ. He would sin in the military sense. He is, therefore, expected to shoot all the more conscientiously because he is a Christian.

Then imagine an episode commonly witnessed after any battle. There is an armistice to bury the dead. Over the broken bodies of their comrades both sides meet in momentary friendship. There is some spiritual communion among the converted ones. What does the scene call to mind? That of an inverted communion service. But the broken body is not that of Christ. It has not sufficed to prevent their fighting.

The command to Christians is "whatsoever ye do, do all to the glory of God." Does participation in these scenes of carnage glorify God? Christ said of the last Paschal feast where the slain Lamb was eaten: "Do this in remembrance of Me." Does that apply to Christian war? Behold the Christian combatants united for a brief moment's peace by the necessity of burying their handiwork—the corpses of their erstwhile bright young comrades. Let us suppose them to have prayer together, and close the service by the usual farewell hymn, "God be with you till we meet again"!

Can it be said to have a Christian answer when they "meet again" on the morrow in the bayonet charge in which they rush upon each other? Why not, if war is Christian? It must be the highest of all religious duties if it be a duty at all. Hallelujahs should be sung after every bloody victory. Angelic songs should mingle with that of these new "Churches triumphant." The holy army of martyrs should join in the paean of praise to Christ the "God of Battles." Let us take a final look at the scene. The bodies have been laid in the earth. The Boer Christians withdraw a few feet, Bibles and hymn books in their hands.

One more ceremony has to be performed by the British Christians. Three volleys must be fired. This time (and this time only) the cartridges are blank. There is no one to kill. What do the three volleys remind us of? Another sacrament: "Go ye into all the world, and preach the gospel to every creature, baptizing them in the name of the Father, the Son, and the Holy Ghost." They have indeed gone into "all the world." They have shot at "every creature," even their spiritual brethren. There have been baptisms of blood and of fire. Men have offered up their lives as if

Blood Against Blood

they had indeed been beforehand "buried with Him by baptism into His death," and no more belonged to themselves, but to Him for His holy war, now represented by these battle-fields. The ceremony solemnizing their passage from life to death must be celebrated by their comrades.

Three volleys are fired as if for the three Persons of the divine Trinity named in the baptismal rite, and then the service is over. Shocking! some one says. And why? If war is so supremely Christian that all must be offered on its red altar, home, family, friends, health, life itself, and if victories must be celebrated by the booming of Christian cannon and the pealing of Christian church bells, then what can be more sacred and holy than the Calvary of a Spion Kop, or more honouring to the Divine Trinity than those three volleys? Should my words be considered more shocking than the facts? There is a Power of Darkness which has ever made the open hand of friendship change into the fist of murder, the beautiful bread-producing grain into the hellish whisky, and turned all the fairest things of God to the foulest uses. Can we not imagine that Power?—to whom Christ declared the Kingdoms of this world belong— could we not fancy him crouching behind the veil and inventing those three parting volleys, with a fiendish irony, as an answer to Christ's "go ye," and His use of the three ever-blessed Names?

"We do not say that it is so. But that he has such schemes is evident from the words of St. Paul, "for we are not ignorant of his devices" (2 Corinthians 2:11). Are "Christian soldiers" to be men who baptise each other into death, for the sake of those Earth Empires, which Daniel and St. John describe by divine command as the Beast powers of Earth? The brain reels when one thinks of all that is involved in the terms Christian soldier and Christian war when thus applied. One seems inclined to inquire: *"Are we standing on our head or on our heels, Everything seems upside down."*

Bear in mind that this book deals exclusively with the duty of men born again, men who "have passed from death unto life," and who "know it" "because they love the brethren." May they accept these lines as a token of true love from one of their brethren. He knows that this is the spirit in which he writes. Drops of both the kinds of blood have fallen upon him as the cover of this book indicates at the base. The truth has cost him all. And he has found it worth infinitely more than that all.

Redeemed Through The Blood

30 declarations of scripture

Under the Law It Was Said:

"The BLOOD shall be for a token upon the houses where ye are." - Exodus 13:13

"When I see the BLOOD I will pass over." - Exodus 13:13

"Moses sprinkled BLOOD upon the people." - Exodus 24:8

"Aaron made atonement with BLOOD." - Exodus 30:10

"It is the BLOOD that maketh the atonement for the soul." -Leviticus 17:11

The LORD JESUS Said:

"This cup is the New Testament in My BLOOD which is shed for you." - Luke 22:20

"This is My BLOOD of the New Testament, which is shed for many for the remission of sins." - Matthew. 24:28

John Said:

"The BLOOD of Jesus Christ cleanseth us from all sin." 1 John 1:7

Blood Against Blood

Peter Said:

"Elect through . . . the sprinkling of the BLOOD of Jesus." - 1 Peter 1:2

"Ye know that ye were not redeemed with corruptible things, but with the precious BLOOD of Christ, as of a lamb without blemish and without spot." - 1 Peter 1:19

"He hath made of one BLOOD all nations of men." Acts 17:26.

(This is true of all men in Adam in creation, and of all the redeemed, in Christ, in redemption.)

"Jesus Christ whom God hath set forth to he a propitiation through faith in His BLOOD." - Romans 3:25

"Being now justified by His BLOOD we shall be saved from wrath." - Romans 5:19

"Guilty of the BLOOD of the Lord." - 1 Corinthians 11:27

"We have redemption through His BLOOD." - Ephesians 1:7

"We are made nigh by the BLOOD of Christ. - Ephesians 1:13

The writer of the Epistle to the Hebrews Said:

"The High Priest went into the second tabernacle not without BLOOD." - Hebrews 9:11

"Having boldness to enter into the holiest by the BLOOD of Jesus." - Hebrews 10:19

"This is the BLOOD of the Testament." - Hebrews 9:20

"He sprinkled with BLOOD the tabernacle." - Hebrews 9:22

"Without shedding of BLOOD there is no remission [or

putting away] of sin." - Hebrews 9:22

"*But ye are come . . . to the BLOOD of sprinkling.*"
Hebrews 12:22 and 24

"*Jesus, that He might sanctify the people with His own BLOOD, suffered without the gate. Let us go forth, therefore, unto Him without the gate, bearing His reproach.*"
Hebrews 13:12 and 13

The REDEEMED in Heaven Say:

"*Unto Him that loved us and washed us from our sins in His own BLOOD, and hath made us kings and priests unto God and His Father, to Him be glory.*" - Revelation 1:5

In the Revelation (the Great Final "Unveilinq") It Is Said:

"*They sung a new song, saying. Thou art worthy, for Thou wast slain, and hath redeemed us to God by Thy BLOOD.*"
Revelation 5:9

"*They washed their robes and made them white in the BLOOD of the Lamb.*" - Revelation 7:4

"They OVERCAME him [Satan] by the BLOOD of the Lamb, and by the word of their testimony, and they loved not their lives unto the death." - Revelation 11:11

"*He was clothed with a vesture dipped in BLOOD.*"
Revelation 19:13

The fate of those who despise the Blood, apart from the cleansing outside the shelter of which there is no salvation. "A certain fearful expectation of judgment . . ." for him "who hath trodden under foot the Son of God, who hath counted the BLOOD of the covenant a common thing. It is a fearful thing to fall into the hands of the living God."
Hebrews 10:27, 29, 31.

CHAPTER NINE

The Lurid Light of Empire

Napoleon promulgated an imperial edict enjoining as great fruitfulness as possible upon the women of France, and giving as the reason that he needed more soldiers. A dignitary of an English Church, in a book published some years ago concerning Africa, congratulated his countrymen on the fact that "our latest protectorate can supply us with as many soldiers as we can ever have occasion to employ." Here we have the modern Christian Empire view of the uses to which the best of its own youth, and of the heathen tribes it conquers, can be put. They will supply us with human flesh as "food for cannon." Does this not savor somewhat of the days of slavery? Must not such sowing of organized iniquity mean some terrible reaping? "We know the price which North America paid in its own blood in its civil war for every slave it had imported from those very regions in former years. It cost a million lives.

The Dutch and the English were the leading nations in the slave trade for a long time. And I observed on looking up the statistics of that trade, that the number of soldiers shipped along the Coast of Africa to the Boer war from North to South, was almost identical with the number of slaves embarked on that very coast, in the same period of time, under the same Christian rule, in a former century, and who crossed the Ocean from East to West!

It is thus that Christianity makes red crosses on a black background on the face of the earth. As I looked at a mass of (mostly beardless) factory lads from Lancashire, packed on the forward deck of a great transport ship at Cork en route for the Boer war, and talked to them from one ship to the other, there was a horrid squeezing at my heart. The scene reminded one of slavery, or the Irish cattle market preceding the shambles. Poor lads ! How hollow their laughter sounded. How shy they looked when I passed them across some religious literature. A shilling a head was their price. The Queen's shilling, taken perhaps outside some corner saloon. And some widow's prodigal boys were probably among them. My heart felt like bursting. So bear with me if this book is very red on very black. It may help show the way to the white for some.

And, Christian brethren, do let us all remember that there is no way from the black of sin to the white of righteousness except through' the red of Calvary. Then why, oh why, should any of us ever consent to lower the value of the blood of Christ as the sole means to a world's salvation by this "Christian" blood shedding? "When will the people of God rouse themselves to recognise that there could be no more successful way of diminishing or destroying the meaning of the blood of the Cross than that of these so-called Christian wars?

The spiritual Christian cannot unite with carnal soldiers without lowering the value on our earth of the very name Christian, and how much more the meaning of the word Christian soldier. It is true that he exalts in equal proportion the apparent value and title of the worldly soldier by his own association with him. He thus falsifies at the same time two opposite values and makes the designations . . .

a **Christian**
a **Worldling**

A Christian have no more apparent value to humanity the one than the other, for they describe men who march together and use precisely the same weapons and methods.

Is not this "watering the stock" of Christianity itself Is it not puffing, booming and falsely inflating the stock of the world, the flesh and the devil? We know how deliberate misrepresenting of values is treated on the Stock Exchange. What right has the Christian to misrepresent the value of his own Master's stock, so to speak, by raising that of the world to the same level?

All this is involved in the adulterated term "Christian soldier." Can Christ be responsible for such confusions? Has our "Lord" designed that His name shall be placed at the head of the prospectus of a bogus Christian company? Such a result would have been worthy of achievement by Satan himself. Men who float companies find it useful to have the name of some lord or highly placed personage at the head of their prospectus as an honorary director. "The Lord Jesus Christ" as Patron and Pounder of these Christian Empire War Companies, armies and expeditions! Can we accept it in silence?

Look again. Christian soldiering? Slavery indeed ! "Love shall conquer." "I promise to love my neighbor (men of every other nation) as myself," and then . . . a button is pressed, and a hidden mine sends a hundred Christian enemies into eternity. Has Love conquered?

If anyone affirms that the bayonet charges of the afternoon or evening of a long day of battle can be made without feelings of anger and hatred, and with philosophical ideas of charity, let him read Sir Conan Doyle on the Boer War, the description of the battle of Mukden, or of the siege of the Embassies in Pekin.

Little wonder that even the English parodied the triumphant telegrams of the Emperor of Germany to his wife praising God for victory, and ordering Te Deums in the national churches. Can we be surprised that they used the terribly sarcastic words: "Ten thousand Frenchmen sent below, Praise God from whom all blessings flow!"

It was hideous but logical. For if the French were so very bad that there was no remedy but to shoot them, and the Germans were so very good as to be the very people for the work, then naturally the ten thousand did "go below." Shooting, like hanging, must mean everything or nothing. All must admit that they are the extreme expression of something. The culminating horror, crime, and impiety of these Christian wars, to which England ships boatloads of her sons, many of them admittedly "prodigal sons," is this, that men seek to justify them by Sinai. "The sword of the Lord" meant "the exceeding sinfulness of sin. "The blood of Christ who voluntarily passed under that sword for us meant the same. To justify these modern wars on Scripture grounds is to destroy the meaning both of Sinai and Calvary at a stroke. Then indeed sin is white and righteousness is black, and the blood of Cain speaks better things than that of Abel.

Then indeed men can waltz, as in the Brussels ball room, all through the Saturday night into the Sunday morning, and on and on into the hellish Sunday carnage of Waterloo, and not even take off their silk stockings and dancing shoes, as did some of the Catholic and Protestant heroes of that battle! Then indeed we may set our faces as flint, and charge on the Christian enemy, mixing in one "Christian soldier's" war song the sanguinary stanzas of the Marseillaise and the songs of Moses and the Lamb, chanted as the Israelites passed up out of the opened grave of the Bed Sea, saved by the blood of the sacrificial offering, the blood of the lamb! Then in one breath we can sing the patriotic line—"Qu'un sang impur abreuve nos sillons," (May our furrows be watered by their impure blood).

And in the next—"There is a fountain filled with blood, Drawn from Immanuel's veins."

What greater proof can we have of the true character of war than the endless amount of argument, yes, and of sophistry, which is required in order to reconcile it in the least degree with the Sermon on the Mount. And if its teachings and the spirit and live^of Christ and the Apostles did not condemn war, how is it that the vast majority of Christians in the first two centuries refused to bear arms? If war is right for Christians, so also are slavery and duelling, for there is no explicit declaration against these in the New Testament. The fact is so plain that he who runs can read:—The whole of the New Testament is opposed to all war, being opposed to the spirit which engenders war, and the whole of the Old Testament is opposed to Christian war because its Mosaic wars were types of the spiritual conflict, just as its sacrificed lambs were types of Christ. The sword when divinely ordered killed unbelievers and Israelitish idolaters equally with the heathen, and its judgments were the outward symbol of the action in the moral sphere of universal Law,* such as the law of Gravitation, which is no respecter of persons.

Those wars expressed the truth, "the soul that sinneth it shall die." Far from justifying our "Christian" war, they all unite to condemn it. Apply their terrible and absolute injunctions to our modern armies, and every unbeliever, every liar, every licentious soldier, every gambling hussar, would have to be killed straight off unless he sought refuge in submission to God, and in shelter under some

66

symbol of Calvary such as were the Jewish sacrifices in their day. Oh! incredible perversion of all the central truths of the Bible, the attempt to justify the horrors of our modern selfish wars by the unselfish religion of a holy God!

Many writers do not hesitate to call war murder. But can the use of this word, which has a specific meaning in the public mind, be applicable so long as the Christian churches and denominations who profess to be the interpreters of God's will, and of the words and work of Christ, approve of war in any shape or form? Until then should not the word be applied (if at all) to them, rather than to the brave men who, in ignorance, and sincerely believing they are doing right, go off to meet grim death on a fair field with no favour. Christ addressed His chief reproaches not to solitary individuals, but to the leaders of the people.

The Scriptures show us that organized sin or apostasy is much worse in the sight of God than are the sins of individuals, committed perhaps in sudden passion or a moral blindness induced by a laxity of principles in the religious, social or governmental strata above them, and the almost incredible want of respect for the Word of God which exists in a day when the word of man in every possible kind of publication is so passionately sought after.

There is something appalling in the distinction which society makes between the killing of a man in heat or anger, or for some unspeakable wrong or outrage of an immoral character against a loved one, and the organized slaying of millions in the wars by which it protects itself, that one cannot wonder that in all countries men, and even women, are taking the law into their own hands and "balancing accounts" with the revolver, as nations do in battle with the machine gun. Society must have speed and despatch in every department today. Is it surprising that "the law's delays" and its uncertainties encourage men to do their own shooting?

And how many are there not who have found secret encouragement in the example given them in war? Governments made their conscience for them. Now they want to make their conscience for themselves, and each' carries a machine gun in his hip pocket. The next step is always anarchy—the imposing of a conscience from below. It is a reaction against selfish force work from above.

How clear then does the destined position of the Christian become amid all this confusion. He cannot countenance the sins of violence either in the wholesale or the retail form, even though his right hand should be nailed to a cross by autocracy, his left by democracy, and his feet by mobocracy, and though Caiaphas should obtain Caesar's help to do away with him. The Christian's place is with the Lamb of God, and not with wolf force in any form. His place in this fallen world is the cross, not the throne, humble service to the last and the least, and not national glory. It is a striking thing that no official was saved at Calvary. The thief on the cross alone. Brutal human "law" had "given him his deserts." He was the most "lost" in the crowd, and so he was the nearest salvation. He was the last of earth, and so he was the first to enter paradise with his Saviour. To keep in the place of the "lost" as regards earthly help and carnal force is the safest spiritually. Conscience must never be sacrificed to a government. We must not kill because emperors order it. The centurion even felt there was something wrong at Calvary. He had killed the Christ in obeying Caesar!

Therefore, even the sins of governments or the united sin of Caiaphas and Caesar, of Church and State, or any form of the unholy alliance of religion and carnal war, cannot justify man in killing his fellow man in battle. No man should ever sell his soul to a ruler.

CHRIST'S CHRISTIANITY
He gives His blood.
He dies to save His own AND His enemies
Making Christians

CANNON CHRISTIANITY
He sheds blood.
He kills in the effort to save his own or himself
Making Infidels

CHAPTER TEN

Where the Lurid Light Leads

So long as such a state of ignorance prevails that Christians can honestly mistake light from below for light from above one must be very careful in the use of terms.

Our Lord said hatred was murder. Let the last word then cover all He put under it. Soldiers shoot out of their rifles that which civilians sometimes feel and say in ordinary life. Far from palliating war, this reveals more clearly its true character. Any dose, small or great, shows what is in a bottle. In this case Christ's words bid us mark it **Deadly Poison.** But the idea of the lawfulness of war for the Christian is handed on, in all sincerity, from generation to generation, without the slightest qualm of conscience, and with each succeeding decade the machinery with which humanity grinds up humanity grows more and more formidable, quick working and complete.

Men pass straight from the quiet and useful industries of our manufacturing districts, from the whirling machinery which deals with our cotton and our corn, to handle machinery on the battlefield, as if fellow-men and fellow-Christians were but corn or cotton, with the difference that the first do not feel and cannot shed blood, and the latter . . . the reader can finish the phrase.

Myself the son of a manufacturer, having learnt to weave and spin with my own hands, having had at one time eleven hundred workmen under my direction, each of whose machines I had been myself trained to run, and having once caught a finger in the cog wheels, I may be able to speak with some knowledge, both of working men and of working machinery. Had you ever heard, as I have, an unearthly shriek ring up through five stories of a huge factory an eighth of a mile in length, and then seen the countless revolving wheels slowing down, while—as the hum of thirty thousand spindles and ten thousand rollers gradually ceased—the shrieks grew louder against the growing stillness; and had you gone down as the responsible manager to find a poor boy lying in a huge heckling machine, with his arm caught in up to the shoulder, the flesh torn off by the countless revolving needles, and had you seen the white awestruck faces gathered round the rescuers, and joined in the quick and careful unbolting of the dread conscienceless machine while the blood dripped, dripped, and the groans died, ever fainter, away, then . . . well, then you would like to do just a little to unbolt some of the machinery of war and set free—even maimed or crippled—some of the poor mothers' sons who have been caught in it!

Surely there is a cry ringing throughout the humming busy world at this hour from a humanity which was, after all, not destined to be ground up in machinery. And if you saw high Christian influence employed to prove that it is all right for our poor factory lads to be taken from before the loom, the spindle or the carder to be shipped in crowds across the world to be put into the machinery and heckled up, while church bells proclaim the victory in the name of the Christ of Calvary, then . . . well, then you would understand such a book as this!

"But," you say, "would we not get into trouble with the governments? "Well, did not Christ do so, and His Apostles? "Were they not put into the machinery? Did they put anyone in?

And if that boy's arm was enough, when caught, to stop, in answer to his awful shriek, that huge factory, surely the body of our Lord should suffice to stop war. For, I repeat, the human body was not designed to get inside machinery, nor the soul either. Shall the sacrifice of Calvary be vain? Meanwhile, all over the Continent of Europe there is rising an even louder protest against war from the humanitarian standpoint, quite apart from that of Christianity. In England the standard book on the New Theology, which has lately appeared, contains but one unanswerable argument against evangelical religion: the awful "Christian" wars which have had its sanction and blessing, and which it has attempted to justify from the Bible.

The writer vanquishes the doctrine of the Blood with apparent ease when he can point to so much "Christian" blood shedding. Should not the war cry of the Church of the Living God at the present hour be "full

CHAPTER ELEVEN

Towards The True Light

There have been moments when some awful war has completed its work of changing a smiling landscape into a howling wilderness, and when the lurid flames are dying out among the smoking ruins—there have been solemn hours like these when even the greatest of our imperial poets and war-song makers seem to have been seized with irresistible spasms of repentance for themselves and their country. The following lines by Rudyard Kipling are intensely significant:

> *"For heathen heart that puts her trust*
> *In reeking tube and iron shard—*
> *All valiant dust that builds on dust,*
> *And guarding calls not Thee to guard—*
> *For frantic boast and foolish word.*
> *Thy Mercy on Thy People, Lord! Amen."*

But there it all ends: in a climax of poetic feeling! And why? Because the root of the matter has not been dealt with. A passing expression of horror at the red fruit of sin cannot suffice. It only creates deeper condemnation by evidencing higher intuitions, unobeyed. Everyone knows that Mr. Kipling, "the poet of the Empire," and his admirers, are ready to encourage and applaud war again at any moment, and that his other war-inspiring songs will still resound in our barracks all along "the thin red line" of our Christian empire, and in the "far flung" outpost. It is understood that such words are not meant to be taken too seriously. They represent a sentiment which can be safely and even appropriately expressed on rare occasions. In this they illustrate the true nature of worldly Christianity.

They are like a cup of the delicate champagne of worldly peace sentiment which can fittingly follow the whisky of war at the close of a banquet of the gods of our era. It is with such passing indulgence in poetic penitence that humanity has deluded itself all along. Its emotions have been affected but its will has not been surrendered to God and truth. It likes to "feel good" now and then and toy with Christianity. All such imperialistic outbursts of piety, however moving or talented, need, therefore, to be examined and classified. They will be found to belong to the sphere which lies on this side of the frontier line of Calvary.

They serve "the god of this world who has blinded the eyes of them who believe not." In the trans-Calvary empire alone can peace be found either for a world or for an individual soul. But those who have been born again alone dwell there. The words "enemy" and "foreigner" are not in their language.

And so the Christian (for I write for our "class" alone) must be for or against war, with all his heart. No half measures are possible for him except he consent to add a deeper darkness to that already surrounding him, by contributing that of a paganized Christianity to existing paganisms. His war work in the world must differ from that of the worldling, otherwise he misleads even them, and helps to make infidels. Nothing can be clearer on this point than the words of our Lord. The terms He uses are always absolute and final.

Darkness or light, life or death, truth or a lie, saving one's life or losing it—heaven or hell—and may we not now, as the summary of His life and teaching add—salvation war or destruction war. Between these extremes He recognized no middle course. "Wherever it was made to exist it was not on His ground. The middle way has always been in reality on Satan's territory. "Ye cannot serve God and Mammon" was His scientific formula.

It is "yea or nay"—whatsoever is more than these " Cometh of the Evil One." It must be so in the question of war. And far from fearing this absoluteness, we should be infinitely thankful for it. It is our one safety. It is the guarantee of our salvation. His word is His bond. His promises fail not. His teaching on matters of life and death must be pellucid to surrendered minds. And thus it cannot be possible that Christ would have purposely left us in doubt and uncertainty upon a vital question like this. He has not. All is clear if we simply take His words at their face value, and with their evident meaning. Too absolute in our obedience to God and our love to men! Men find true Christianity too absolute! And yet what Christian objects to have absolute eggs for breakfast 1 Whence then come the complications which people see in this matter? Simply from want of uttermost surrender to God. In religion, spiritual complications and difficulties only appear when we "love our lives," and seek some broader way than that of the yea and nay.

Spiritual fog comes from the spirit of compromise and from want of consecration. This accounts for the calmness the martyrs experienced when right up against death.

What is the force of an earthly regiment? Its entire surrender to the service of King and country. The men conquer because they are willing to die. This is what brings them into closest contact with the enemy in the bayonet charge, into the place where they can kill. The same is true of the apostolic Christian. He gets into the closest contact with the "enemy," because he is determined to save even should he get killed in the attempt. How awful then that Christian lives of such salvation value should be thrown away in these hideous wars of Earth Empire.

Is then the Blood of their redemption so cheap? Can their lives produce so little for Christ? And are there not always sufficient worldlings to be found to do the war and the killing without Christians, God's "little flock," being dragged into the work?

Are not out-and-out, what-care-I Christians the only sort who can win to Christ the desperate anarchist, or lead to repentance the Parisian Apache or the Yorkshire rough who howls "knock 'em down till a fettle 'em with ma hoof," as I heard one say? How often has the writer seen this truth illustrated on the Continent, in the conversion of those most violently hostile to all religion, and who as a consequence had never come into personal contact with ministers of the gospel. But when they were sought out by men as desperate as themselves, at the opposite pole of effort, and when they rushed upon them with knives, oaths and blows, then they were converted by the shock of hatred against love, and grace against the "law" of steel. And so we are "left without excuse." If we take Calvary and Christianity seriously the whole question is settled in an instant. Sincerity is all that is required. Unshakable uprightness of heart makes duty clear. Christ gave Himself for us. We give ourselves for humanity. We do exactly what the worldly soldiers do in their wars. We sacrifice our lives if need be but we kill no one. All complications disappear once this point is made plain. It seems so simple that it appears childish to say it. In this it resembles the whole plan of salvation by grace.

For most men the gospel is "too good to be true." To some for the same reason the preaching of the cross is foolishness. The gospel is too simple, too absolute, too instantaneous in its effects, too complete, too "whosoever" to be accepted by minds which have lived in the fogs of the world's policies, compromises and calculations. It is extreme. So also is worldly war. This kills right off. The other saves right off.

And before it can save the last and the least it, too, must be extreme. In other words it must be true to itself. It has one message and one only, for the loftiest of earth's emperors and the lowest of earth's cutthroats. It asks nothing of either. It neither flatters the one in his high-class sins, nor despises the other for his low-class "crimes." It is even, if anything, nearer a crucified thief than an enthroned Caesar. The greater the need the greater its readiness with the SPIRITUAL remedy, the only one it has got for the world's woes.

Such men are valuable, though the world has ever made them the off-scouring of all things. If in modern days the bloody cross is too vulgar for refined and civilised sin to use in martyrizing the true followers of Christ, it has endless weapons of misrepresentation, calumny and isolation, by which to secure their moral assassination.

But to remain ever "lost" will be their salvation. You can take nothing from nothing. What the world needs is a body of men not afraid to die, who are determined to owe it nothing, and who will not let their roots become so deeply fastened into its vested interests that their spiritual life will be compromised by any obligations not to disturb its false peace, or its real war. Here we reach the centre of the whole question of the lawfulness of war for the Christian.

Blood Against Blood

And if Europe can find and "keep" eleven millions of men ready to "leave all" at a day's notice, to cross land and sea to die in killing others—cannot God find and keep a little flock of disciples willing to suffer in order to save? And when He gets them shall they or can they be mixed with the other soldiers in their wars?

Let us be Christian soldiers.

In this connection, I reprint here a few verses, written some years ago, and which appeared in *The Friend* . . .

THE KING OF LIFE AND LOVE

There is a King whose glory

Thrives not on human pain,
Whose Kingdom's hallowed story

Knows not oppression's reign.

The sword of law has smitten
This gentle King of grace,

And Wisdom's hand has written:
"He suffered in our place."

For subjects in transgression

His Cross to Heaven appeals,
His wounds make intercession.

And by His stripes He heals;
The prisoners He releases,

All debts His blood can pay.
Our sins and our diseases

The Lamb has borne away.

Then whence war's surging sorrow.

Blood Against Blood

Its wildly clashing arms.
Its harrowing to-morrow,

Its torturing alarms?
Is it from earth's Sin-Bearer,

This fierce self-righteous sits
And is His crown the fairer

For bloody fights men win?
These grim hosts, do they "follow

The Lamb where'er He goes,"
With voices hoarse and hollow

Do cannon bless our "foes 1"
Are they the gospel sounding:

"To men goodwill and peace,"
And is it "grace abounding"

When armaments increase?

Nay! is it not the rather

Denial of His cross.
Who came from God the Father

To suffer every loss,
That we might find salvation

And life and peace regain
Through One by His own nation

Despised, rejected, slain?

CHAPTER TWELVE

Spying and Lying

With some difficulty I have succeeded in obtaining a worn and moldy copy of a book, now out of print by Major General Sir Garnet Wolseley, G.C.M.G., K.C.B. titled "The Soldier's Pocket Guide to Field Service. It must be remembered in perusing the following extracts, that the author was for a considerable time the Commander-in-Chief of the British Army, and that his words are therefore the expression of the highest authority in the land on militarism, and its morals. They are commands binding upon the conscience of every young man, fresh from a Sunday School or from confirmation in some Christian church. There he learned that lying was a vice. Here he learns that it is a virtue. There he was taught the Scriptures, which gave him to understand that it was better to die than to lie. Here he is told that it is obligatory to lie, not only in order not to die himself, but that he can the better cause the dying of multitudes of the enemy—"Christians" also perhaps.

At his mother's knee, at school and at church, he was "bred up to feel it a disgrace even to succeed by a falsehood." Here such teaching concerning truth is treated as "pretty little sentences which will do for a child's copy book."

Viscount Wolseley is honest in describing how this systematized dishonesty will not suit the true Christian. He shows that therefore these hosts which kill are no place for him. *"The man who acts upon these [elementary principles of truth] had better sheathe his sword for ever."* But the fact remains that some sincere Christians do become soldiers. Let them therefore be forewarned.

They, with their fellows, are perhaps about to be hurled in masses against the cannon and the bayonets of the "enemy." They are about to be killed in killing. To prepare for this climax they must make the supreme sacrifice, must die to truth. They must live to die. They must surrender their consciences to this new commander of body and soul. He must, to them, take the place of Christ. He is the final arbiter of their destiny. That is what it really comes to.

What, therefore, is the logic of the position? To commit the outward culminating act of their existence in the bayonet charge where they will lose their bodily life they must first stifle the voice of truth and love within. The one is the natural consequence of the other. Can it be therefore certain that war can be absolutely Christian when it first of all blows up the rock foundation of Christianity—truth? Christians can not afford to risk themselves in uncertainties where vital matters are concerned. If war is not certain to be right they must not engage in it.

Lord Wolseley says:

> *"As a nation we are bred up to feel it a disgrace even to succeed by falsehood; the word spy conveys something as repulsive as slave; we will keep hammering along with the conviction that 'honesty is the best policy,' and that truth always wins in the long run. These pretty little sentences do well for a child's copy-book, but the man who acts upon them in war had better sheathe his sword for ever. Spies are to be found in every class of society, and gold, that mighty lever of men, is powerful enough to unlock secrets that would otherwise remain unknown at the moment. An English general must make up his mind to obtain information as he can, leaving no stone unturned in order to do so."*

In reading the following extract concerning the class of men to be employed as spies, and in observing the calculation that in this work you may expect an output in reliable information of only ten per cent. —we must bear in mind that in the armies of the new ally of Britain— Japan, spies are often Colonels, Majors, and Captains, and spying is considered by these, our future co-workers, as a most honourable employment:

> *"The management of spies is difficult; out of every ten employed, you are fortunate if one gives you truthful*

Information. It is important that spies should be unknown to one another. Care should be taken to make each believe that he is the only one employed. Some serve for patriotism, others for money, some receive pay from both sides; if such a one can be depended upon, he is invaluable. All should be petted and made a great deal of, being liberally paid and large rewards given them when they supply any really valuable information. A few thousand pounds is of no consequence to a nation, but if well laid out in obtaining information, it may be the indirect means of adding to the victories of one's country. It is very necessary that all bona-fide spies should always have about their persons some means of proving themselves really to be whom they represent: a certain coin of a certain date, a Bible of a certain edition, a Testament with the third or seventh leaf torn out, etc., etc."

It is significant that the third or seventh leaf of the New Testament falls almost in all cases within the limits of the Sermon on the Mount. But I do not think this accuracy of absolute contrast was meant by Sir Garnet as supreme irony. However, happening accidentally, it is doubly significant, and doubly ironical, by the association it establishes. There is another expression which must be painfully discordant to the true Christian:

Lord Wolseley says: "As a nation we are bred, etc.," thereby implying that hitherto we have been as a nation more scrupulous in truthfulness than some others, and that therefore special care must be taken with young Englishmen, in rooting out from their consciences all remaining habits of truthfulness, that they may be the better fitted for wars of destruction. In other words to become good soldiers they must become bad Christians. Could anything constitute a more complete giving away of the whole case for "Christian wars"? Would it be possible to make a more unblushing defence of the systematized Jesuitism which has lain at the back of the military system, as adapted to Christian nations, ever since the time of Constantine?

Not only must the individuality be sunk in the huge machine, and each Christian become but a number in the marching, maneuvering mass, but that number must be taught that lying is loyalty, if it appear to be useful to the national cause, and that it is true devotion to "God and country" to do evil that good may come.*

One could naturally multiply the examples of these maxims and principles, so inseparable from war, by quotations from Continental military instructors. Take the following honest declaration of an Austrian officer. Bear in mind that his empire is the hereditary representative of "the Holy Roman Empire," created under Papal patronage after the fall of the old Pagan Empire of Rome. "The recruit brings with him common moral notions, of which he must seek immediately to get rid.

For him victory, success must be everything. The most barbaric tendencies in men come to life again in war, and for war's uses they are incommensurably good ! Far better is it for an army to be too savage,too cruel, too barbarous, than to possess too much sentimentality and human reasonableness. If the soldier is to be good for anything as a soldier, he must be exactly the opposite of a reasoning and thinking man. The measure of goodness in him is his possible use in war. "War, and even peace, require of the soldier absolutely peculiar standards of morality."

Lest the declaration, above quoted, be not clear to some, let us put the thought in another form: The better a man is as a Christian, the more "useless" he must be as a soldier. The converse would then be true also as regards the gospel war. Reverse the argument and see.

Truly we might add the covenant, "honesty (in military precepts) is the best policy." Let us be thankful that such loyal declarations are forthcoming to help tear from before the eyes of young Christians who are enrolling themselves under earthly flags, this moral bandage which all unconsciously to many is being placed upon them.

Refused To Bear Arms

Not till about three centuries after our Lord's ministry, when Christianity began to become "popular," and was advancing towards the questionable position of being the State Religion, did Christians begin to bear arms.

Here is the testimony of some of the early "Fathers":

1. As regards the principle.

> **Justin the Martyr**, in the second century, says: "The devil is the author of all war."

> **Tatian & Clemens of Alexandria** spoke the same.

> **Tertullian** wrote: "Jesus Christ, by disarming Peter, disarmed every soldier afterwards, for custom never sanctions an illicit act." And he further writes: "Can one who professes the peaceful doctrine of the Gospel be a soldier, when it is his duty not so much as to go to law?"

> And again: "Our religion teaches us that it is better to be killed than to kill."

> **Cyprian** declares war, like all other Pagan customs of his times, to be repugnant to the spirit and letter of the Gospel. It is he who seems to have first asked of the whole world the unanswerable question: "Why is it that when a single murder is committed, it is deemed a crime, but that this crime shall be a virtue if multitudes are slaughtered?"

83

Lactantius, the next eminent writer in order of time after Cyprian, says: "It can never be lawful for a righteous man to go to war, whose warfare is in righteousness itself." And again: "It can never be lawful to kill a man, whose person the Divine Being designed to be sacred as to violence."

Oeigen, Ambrose, Chetsostom, Jerome, and **Cyril** gave it also as their several opinions that it was unlawful for Christians to go to war.

2. As regards the practice and the facts.

There is no instance on record of Christians entering into the army for the first two centuries. On the other hand, they declined the military profession as one in which it was not lawful for them to engage.

Tertullian, in describing the period between 170 and 200, and alluding to certain of the great armies of Rome, which composed about half the entire forces of the empire, says that no Christians were to be found in all these armies.

Justin the Martyr and **Tatian**, in their writings, make clear distinctions between "soldiers" and "Christians."

Clemens of Alexandria gives the Christians who were contemporary with him the appellation of "peaceables," or of "the followers of peace," thus distinguishing them from the soldiers of the age, and he says expressly that "those who were the followers of peace used none of the instruments of war."

Ibenaeus, who lived about the year 180, affirms that the famous prophecy of Isaiah had been fulfilled in his time; "for the Christians," said he, "have changed their swords and their lances into instruments of peace, and they know not how to fight."

Celsus, who lived at the end of the second century, attacked the Christian religion. He made it one of his charges against the Christians that they refused in his time to bear arms for the Emperor, even in the case of supposed necessity. He told them further, "that if the rest of the empire were of their opinion, it would soon be overrun by the barbarians."

Oeigen, in his answer to **Celsus**, admits the facts to be as stated by the latter, namely, that the Christians would not bear arms, and he justifies them for refusing the practice, on the principle of the unlawfulness of war.

Tertullian in his "Soldier's Garland," says that many in his time, immediately on their conversion, quit the military service.

Aechelaus, who lived about the year 280, left it on record that many Roman soldiers who had embraced Christianity, after having witnessed the fearless faithfulness of Marcellus, who refused to take up arms, immediately did the same.

Eusebius declares also that about the same time "numbers laid aside a military life and became private persons rather than abjure their religion. ' ' Are we not therefore justified in summing up in their own answer the entire testimony of the first three hundred years of Christianity in the words of Marcellus, Maximilian, Cassian, and others, brave soldiers: who were too brave to be soldiers of anyone but Christ "I am a Christian, and therefore I cannot fight."

CHAPTER FOURTEEN

What is War
some options

John Wesley "Shall Christians assist the Prince of Hell, who was a murderer from the beginning, by telling the world of the benefit or the need of war?"

Dr. Adam Clarke "War is as contrary to the spirit of Christianity as murder."

Bishop Fraser "War is not the triumph of righteousness. It is the triumph of brute force. Can anything be conceived more unchristian, more irrational, than the present mode by which international quarrels are commonly adjusted?"

George Fox (when offered a captaincy). "I cannot fight, for the spirit of war is slain within me."

Robert Barclay "It is as easy to obscure the sun at midday, as to deny that the primitive Christians renounced all revenge and war." (See story of his father, Col. Barclay, in appendix.)

Dr. Chalmers "The mere existence of the prophecy 'they shall learn war no more,' is a sentence of condemnation on war."

Robert Hall "War is nothing less than a temporary repeal of the principles of virtue."

Sydney Smith "God is forgotten in war: every principle of Christianity is trampled upon."

John Bright "Force is no remedy."

Blood Against Blood

Duke of Wellington (to Lord Shaftesbury) "War is a most detestable thing. If you had seen but one day of war, you would pray God that you might never see another."

General Sherman (U.S.A.) "War is hell."

The following examples of individual faithfulness may be added:

> **John Clibborn** (Irish Civil "War, 1689). When threatened with death refused to defend himself. Said war was against his Christian principles. The pistol missed fire twice when his death was attempted. Rebel officer ordered his men to desist, saying Mr. Clibborn was a Quaker and under Divine protection.
> They burned his house down. It had been a refuge for the wounded of both armies. (See appendix.) Previous to his conversion he had been a military leader.

> **Abraham Shackleton** (Irish Rebellion, 1798). "The rebels took us out and said if we would not fight we should stop a bullet. I told them that as to myself I felt quite undisturbed, I had no displeasure against them. They acted in ignorance. They might
> put me to death, as I was in their hands, but they would never persuade me to use any act of violence against my fellow men!"

> **John Nelson** (1740). Stone mason, Methodist preacher, companion of the Wesleys. When press ganged, to stop his fearless preaching: "I shall not fight; for I cannot bow my knee before the Lord to pray for a man and then get up and kill him when I have done."

CHAPTER FIFTEEN

What Say The Scriptures

IS war right or wrong; a blessing or a curse; a duty or a sin? What say the scriptures?

War, by which a human being (whose soul, according to our Lord's word, is worth more than a world) is suddenly smitten down by his fellow-man, and his spirit launched into eternity, is something of such are extreme and absolute character that it cannot be partially right or partially wrong; it must be the one or the other, definitely and absolutely. Life and death are extreme things. To love your neighbor as yourself, or to pass a bayonet through his chest, may be safely looked upon as being opposites. "To save life or to destroy it" are not things bearing much resemblance. Between converting a man and killing him there certainly lies a considerable distance.

The object of the following questions and answers is to present in a concise form the Scripture argument against blood-shedding war, and thus submit to some young Christian, campaigning, or in barracks, or on the point of enrolling, information which may help him to decide for himself what are our Lord's marching orders as regard carnal war. Let it be remembered that I deal with this question from the standpoint of Christianity alone, and am speaking chiefly to those who have become Christians by spiritual regeneration, or what is generally termed conversion; to those who have received the knowledge of the forgiveness of their sins by repentance and faith in Christ and His Blood, and who have been given, by the Spirit, the assurance that they have become children of God.

You consider all blood-shedding war by Christians to be wrong?

Yes, absolutely.

89

On what do you base this conviction?

On the Word of God, as given in the Old and New Testaments, upon the fact that Christ our King shed His Blood to stop all sin, and therefore all bloodshedding, and upon the very spirit of Christianity.

What are the principal passages of Scripture which may be quoted in support of this view?

"Thou Shalt not kill!" (Exodus 10:13)

This passage must include every form of bloodshedding, except when a definite order to the contrary has been given by God. The wars of the Old Testament and the death sentences pronounced and executed upon those rebelling against the Divine Law, were part of God's direct government on earth. They were Divine Judgments, anticipating to a certain degree the scenes of the great Judgment Day. They were pronounced and executed upon those who, by numberless outward manifestations of God's miraculous power and authority, were left "without excuse."

The "Thou shalt not kill" was accompanied in the Old Testament dispensation by a definite "Thou shalt kill," and all the cases to which this command became applicable were described in a manner to leave no doubt possible.

These material judgments were the awful counterpart of the mighty material manifestations of God's glory, and of His will and power. In other words, they were the counterpart of a continual succession of miracles. The sword of the "Thou shalt kill" kept pace with indescribably mighty deeds, such as the plagues of Egypt, the dividing of the Red Sea, and with such scenes as those of Mount Sinai, the giving of the heavenly miraculous commissariat of manna, the water bursting from the smitten rock, and the earthquakes suddenly confirming the words of judgment pronounced by the High Priest. Those executions and wars were the necessary accompaniment of the theocracy on earth, and so carefully did the Almighty guard the minds of His people from the danger of confounding His judgments—definitely and specially commanded to them—from such carnal and selfish wars as those of the present day, that He obliged all His soldiers and armies to be ever ready, at an instant's notice, to he reduced to absolute helplessness. It was so before the walls of Jericho, when one shout of faith was all the effort allowed to the entire host wherewith to lay low those walls.

Where is the modern Christian army that would be willing to put itself under such a discipline as that? Where is the modern Christian General or Government that would prescribe, like Gideon, the immediate reduction of the forces by nine-tenths? Where is the modern Christian army marching behind an Ark of Divine Covenant that can divide a river, make heathen idols fall to earth before it, or slay a man who touches it, in carnal fear for its safety?

It seems almost incredible that Christians can be found at the present day to seriously argue in favour of modern wars between Christian nations, by reasonings based upon the Jewish theocracy, and the doings of those armies of old who lived in an atmosphere of perpetual and gigantic miracle. Can it therefore be denied that we have a right to inscribe in flaming red letters across the track of young Christians who leave the Sunday School, the local preachers' platform, or the pulpit, to go half round the world to dynamite fellow-Christians to pieces, or to spear their chests across, the solemn command: "Thou Shalt not kill"?

But are there not passages in the New Testament which would seem to authorize or to command war for the Christians? Yes, perhaps, if separated from the context, or if misinterpreted, but not otherwise. Men are warned against "wresting the Scriptures, to their own destruction"; surely, therefore, they can also wrest them to the destruction of others, or to the double destruction of the double fratricide represented by modern Christian war.

Such words as "He that hath no sword, let him sell his garment and buy one"; "The magistrate . . . beareth not the sword in vain" (the mere statement of a fact), have been, it is true, used to contradict the whole of Christ's teaching upon war.

Let it suffice here to give that supreme command of our Lord to Peter, the leader of the disciple band: "Put up thy sword into its sheath, for they that take the sword shall perish by the sword."

91

Will you give some other passages which definitely forbid war?

Can it be denied that the following texts condemn, not only blood-shedding wars as being anti-Christian, but also the very spirit and disposition which leads to such wars:

"Whatsoever ye would that men should do unto you, do ye unto them" (Matthew 7:12)

"Resist not evil" (Matthew 5:39)

"If anyone shall smite thee on the one cheek, turn to him the other also" (Matthew 5:39)

"Love your enemies; bless them that curse you, do good to them that hate you, and pray for them who despitefully use you and persecute you, that ye may be the children of your Father which is in Heaven, for He maketh His Sun to rise on the evil and the good" (Matthew 5:35)

"For if ye love them which love you, what reward have ye?" (Luke 6:46)

"Be ye therefore perfect, even as your Father in Heaven is perfect" (Matthew 5:38 to end of chapter).

"The weapons of our warfare are not carnal, but spiritual" (2 Corinthians 10:4)

"We war not after the flesh" (Ephesians 6:12)

"We wrestle not with flesh and blood" (Ephesians 6:12)

"If My Kingdom were of this world, then would My servants fight" (John 18:36)

"Bless them which persecute you; bless, and curse not" (Matthew 5:44)

"Recompense to no man evil for evil" (Romans 12)

"Avenge not yourselves" (Romans 12:19)

"If thy enemy hunger, feed him; if he thirst, give him drink: for in so doing thou shalt heap coals of fire upon his head" (Romans 12:20)

"Be not overcome of evil, but overcome evil with good" (Romans 12:21)

"Love worketh no ill to his neighbor, therefore love is the fulfilment of the law" (Romans 12 and 13)

What law, then, do these indescribably awful Christian wars fulfil? None, surely, but the law of pride, of hatred, and of hell.

"From whence come wars and fighting? Come they not from your lusts, which war in the flesh?" (James 5:1)

God's Word requires nothing to support it. Faith and obedience simply consist in recognizing this fact without reserve, and acting upon it.

Surely the foregoing quotations are more than sufficient to settle the mind of any Christian as to his duty in this matter. In their presence how can it be possible for him to assume that his duty lies in exactly the opposite direction, and that it can be for him an imperative obligation to slay some fellowman—yes, and even some fellow-Christian—and to offer up his own life in the effort to do so? Could fanaticism go further than that? And yet it is probable that there are multitudes who would esteem such a book as this to represent fanaticism, and not the endless and inexpressibly awful blood-shedding, in which men place a vain fanatical hope of the coming of the golden era of our world.

Must it not honour Christ for a Christian to stand out alone in face of one of these mighty modern hosts as one of His "lambs" under the fire of their "wisdom's" scorn as he refuses to wield their weapons?

But what of the words "render unto Caesar the things that are Caesar's, and unto God the things which are God's"?

The utmost that anyone can adduce from this passage in favour of war, is that the body born within the bounds of an empire must, if needs be, be surrendered to the sovereign at his call. But that is precisely what the Christian does, in allowing himself to be shot down by his king's orders rather than shoot. He does not resist Caesar bodily, or seek to kill him to save his own life or even to preserve himself or his fellows from military service, or from the tyranny of an autocratic government.

He is not a revolutionary. He thus surrenders his body to Caesar and his spirit to God. He would surrender body and soul to Caesar in going to war. By dying rather than disobey the command of Christ "put up thy sword," he not only renders his spirit to God but by "sowing" his body as a martyr, does perhaps "a hundredfold more" to serve the gospel cause, and exemplify its principles, than had he been able to live and preach the Gospel. Take the opposite case. A regiment is charging upon the enemy. How is the Christian soldier to explain to his comrades that he is rushing with bared bayonet on the foe from opposite motives to theirs, and in obedience to Christ the Prince of Peace and of love? If he cannot do so, the weight of his example is thrown on to the "Cain" side of the balance rather than the "Christ" side. And infidels, who have at the bottom a shrewd idea of what the gospel involves, would require much explanation indeed to make his action appear to them the supreme expression of his loyalty to Christ.

This is no casuistry—but simple logic.

Can you explain the words of Christ to His disciples: "He that hath no sword let him sell his garment and buy one" (Luke 222:36) ?

Let us notice the extreme character of the expression used by our Lord: "He that hath no sword let him sell his garment and buy one." Are those who see in this passage an authorisation or a command to sustain the armies of their country, willing for all the logical consequences to which this will lead them?

(1) Their country is to be set so much higher in their esteem than property or life, that, having sold their home, furniture, and all but their clothes, they are to sell their coat to buy a sword.

(2) And who is to decide with the certainty necessary for such an extremity, which is the party to be thus served in case where a country is changing by a revolution from a monarchical to a republican form of government or vice versa? In the Old Testament wars the certainty of God's will in the matter was always given. The wars were part of His rule, not of man's. Gentile wars are not. The Israelites were obliged to seek His guidance before engaging in either defensive or offensive war, that the entire question might be one of His glory and Kingdom rather than theirs. Their war, against outward enemies and wicked nations, were types of the Christian's inward war for the extermination of spiritual enemies, just as the outward circumcision was a type of the circumcision of the heart, and the Jewish sacrifices prefigured the sacrifice of Christ for our sins. They also foreshadowed the war of evangelization and missionary effort. God's outward kingdom on earth no longer exists.

If therefore Christ's words apply to carnal swords and not spiritual, to Gentile government and not Jewish, then every Christian who is a subject of the Sultan of Turkey is bound in obedience to Christ to sell his very coat in order to defend the Monarch spoken of in England as "the assassin of the Armenian Christians," against the "Christian" armies which might invade his country, to force him to cease persecuting his non-Mohammedan subjects.

But if the "sword" be here taken as spiritual, then the expression will be found to fall into its place naturally as one of a series: "If thine eye offend thee pluck it out." Does a Christian pluck out his physical eye at conversion or renounce the "lust of the eye"? "If any man will be my disciple let him sell all that he hath." Is an auction the necessary prelude to every conversion? And if a Christian be entering upon a time of fierce trial of his faith and consecration, what would be more natural than to say, "arm yourself spiritually at all costs"?

Christians who here demand the literal interpretation of the word "sword" ought to realize what a charge they lay at the door of their Lord and Master, namely, that He was either mocking at His disciples or wilfully deluding them, for unless He meant to multiply the swords by miracle, as He did the bread, one could not imagine Him thinking that two were enough with which to overcome the Roman legions. Insistence on a literal interpretation thus borders on blasphemy, in attributing to Christ fanatical folly, or deception. Do not the words of protest against Peter's use of the sword, and the command to sheathe it, preclude all possibilities of misunderstanding?

"Thinkest thou that I cannot now pray to my Father, and He shall presently give me more than twelve legions of angels." (Matthew 26:53)

But have not Christian wars been raging for many hundreds of years?

Yes, they commenced when Christianity began to be Paganized, and it seems almost incredible that the chief seal of their "lawfulness," set upon them by history (yes, and quoted by sincere Christian historians), is that absurd and monstrous legend of the vision of the Roman Emperor Constantine, who was supposed to have seen a flaming cross hanging in the sky above his murdering legions, and who interpreted it into an order to become a Christian,—and a fighting one! Is it possible that such fables still find credence?

But did not the early Christians in the days of Pentecost, in the times of the Apostles, march and fight under the Roman eagles?

No! The conversion of any who were soldiers was generally immediately marked by the laying down of their arms. In some cases they stepped forth before the ranks of their comrades and did it publicly. They preferred to be run through, or to be cast to the lions in the Coliseum rather than kill their fellow-men.

But did not some of the Reformers and thousands of their followers fight, and are there not thousands of clergymen and preachers to-day who declare war to he a Christian duty?

Yes. We are still but half emerged from the darkness of the middle ages. There are still to be found dear Christians who have time and energy in the midst of a dying world for balls, theatres, and worldly entertainments. Can we imagine that it was so with the Christians of Pentecost, and with the glorious host of "overcomers" described in the Book of Revelation?

But many of the Reformers saw clearly the truth concerning so-called Christian war. "They who defend war must defend the dispositions leading to war, and these dispositions are absolutely forbidden by the Gospel." So says Erasmus, and further: "Since the time that Jesus said, 'Put up thy sword into its scabbard' (Matthew 26:22), Christians ought not to go to war. Christ suffered Peter to fall into an error in this, so that when he put up Peter's sword he might not remain any longer in doubt that war was prohibited." That is plain language, is it not?

Wycliff, says Priestley, seems to have thought it wrong to take the life of a man on any account, and that war was utterly unlawful.

It is not so long ago since the cause of Slavery was advocated with passionate energy by the great majority of Christians in America, in England and in its Colonies. These countries held countless slaves in bondage, and actually justified their actions by quotations (garbled of course) from Scripture.

But might not the consequences be very serious to life and property if we were all to put in practice such commands as those you have quoted?

Yes, certainly, but there is not a word in the Bible to say that we are to preserve our lives or our property by any wrong means, or that we are to hesitate for one moment to offer them to the service of the Kingdom of God, or to lose them if needs be in that Blessed Service. Christians are treated in the Bible as the loyal subjects of the King of Heaven. "We live in a rebel, and therefore a fallen world, and should thus consider ourselves as liable at any moment to be martyred. Their only right to existence at all is based on the Redemption wrought out in the tragedy of Gethsemane and Calvary, and the shedding of Jesus' blood. They are bought up, redeemed, therefore they are free and happy, for they are not their own. This is their elementary everyday conviction, and they are in a condition at any moment to do and suffer anything for the "Will of God, to go anywhere, to do everything which may be necessary for the salvation of man, and which disinterested Love, Truth and Self-sacrifice may command, knowing that Divine Providence watches over them, and that nothing can happen to them unless permitted by God and overruled to their true good and that of humanity at large. But are not these wars necessary for the spread of civilization and the opening up of heathen countries? Yes, if we could consider that organized lying or theft would be necessary.

It is quite true that God's people use the roads made by Empires. God used a Roman ship to take Paul to the shores of Italy and a Roman road to take him to the capital. This is part of the indirect providential administration of God, which is quite distinct from His direct administration resulting from obedience to His laws in the lives of His true subjects. God, indirectly, by the laws of chemistry, makes the powder explode in the pistol of the assassin. But is it God who has committed the murder ?

As a matter of fact, the refined and limitless selfishness, the nameless vices, the passions, and corruptions of modern "Christianity" and modern civilization rush far more quickly and in infinitely greater torrents over the bone-made roads of Empires in heathen lands than do the tides of missionary effort.

There exists a much better way for those who go to war to manifest their "interest in the spread of civilization"; for instance, let one-tenth or one hundredth or one-thousandth part of those who go to shoot and to be shot down give themselves up with similar zeal and courage, and with the same utter forgetfulness of danger and death, to carry the Gospel of Christ to the heathen: that would be consistent and honest.

But do you think war will he abolished by Christianity at its present rate of progress?

No. But that has nothing to do with our individual duty.

One of the most glorious and solemn parts of the programme of Christianity is that the King is soon coming to claim the Throne of the World. He is coming to reign on or over earth with His glorified body, and with the multitudes who will be with Him to share His Life, Light, and Glory. That is part of the common elementary faith of Christianity. Those who hold this apparently (to the world) fanatical belief are even considered by some of their brethren as faddists or visionaries, nevertheless their hope is part of Christianity's glorious programme, just as much as is faith and love.

Blood Against Blood

"We appear to be now well on into the Saturday night of the world, Saturday night in Christian nations is the most drunken time of the week. We need not be surprised if, as we approach the end, spiritual, moral, and intellectual drunkenness will abound in Christendom to an extraordinary extent.

"We are not of the night. Let us watch and be sober." "They that are drunken are drunken in the night." When night settles down definitely on an individual, a community, or a world, we may expect to witness the fulfilment of the Word of God, that various kinds of drunkenness will abound. This will be true even of Christian Churches and Associations, as well as of Christian Empires! They will have recourse to ever more powerful carnal *stimulants*. They that are drunken are DRUNKEN in the night.

CHAPTER SIXTEEN

Unregenerate and Fallacious

There exists a widespread and ever-extending anti-military movement on the Continent of Europe. It is non-Christian, political, partly social-democratic, partly anarchistic. It is an extension to the present social conditions and an application of the principles underlying the French Revolution.

The working classes claim that they pay most in blood and labour to support war, and that the middle and upper classes profit most by it.

This anti-war movement is thus a declaration of war in another form, —war between the masses and the classes. It has nothing to do with Christianity. Its "peace principles" must not, therefore, be con- founded with those of the gospel of Christ, nor its anti-militarism with that of primitive and pure Christianity. This book is not anti-military in the ordinary sense. It is simply pro-Christian.

The first is merely negative, and therefore productive of as little good to humanity as is war—that other supreme expression of mere negation. It is opposed to wars of destruction simply because it advocates the war of Salvation, and believes it to be the only true remedy to the ills from which fallen humanity suffers. It is loyal to all kings alike in being loyal to the King of kings, who "came not to destroy men's lives, but to save them."

It centres around the truth that the blood shed on Calvary obviates all further blood-shedding by Christians. For it would be futile and offensive to lay down any law or rule of conduct for worldlings. Sin and worldliness have their own invariable and inevitable laws. One of these is that the work of sin is war, and the wages of sin is death. Its opposite is the divine law: "the work of righteousness shall be peace, and the effect of righteousness quietness and assurance for ever." It is folly to ask any creatures, human or non-human, to submit themselves to any other laws than those which naturally belong to their sphere —the "world" in which they live. It would be folly to ask worldlings to accept Christian peace principles while living in a state of sin, rebellion and war against God. It is folly to expect the brotherhood of man to be recognized in practice, till the Fatherhood of God has been first restored among them. This restoration can alone take place by the new birth into the family of God. Through Calvary by the blood of Christ, and by His resurrection-life alone can this regeneration be experienced.

But these principles of pardon, life and peace through the blood of Christ are the exact opposite of the principles of hatred, war and death, which must underlie all the systems by which fallen men seek to remedy the ills under which the world is labouring. Hence also worldly systems of peace being based,—equally with those of war,—upon armed force must be similarly illusory. They are equally represented in the words of our Lord: "If the blind lead the blind, both shall fall into the ditch."

False remedies only increase the disease by setting up fresh irritation in the system. False hopes lead to violent reaction and multiplied fears. False peace invariably engenders real war. The temporary suppression or compression of sin only causes an increase of its explosive force. Sin can never be its own remedy. Corruption can never be its own cure. The drowning man cannot have himself by taking hold of his own hair. The drunken man cannot wheel himself home in a barrow.

Lost and fallen man can no more be his own saviour at the end than he could have been his own creator at the beginning. There is no salvation elsewhere than at the cross, where the God-man gave Himself for His creatures, and restored from the heavenly side the bridge which man had broken down from the earthly side, and could never reconstruct across the abyss, were he to build towers of Babel without end.

True Christianity is alone true science, because it deals with causes, not effects, with roots, not fruits. It removes sin instead of merely suppressing it. It cleanses it away instead of gilding it over. It destroys war by destroying the spirit which engenders war.

All peace principles, therefore, which are not absolutely Christian, are absolutely illusory, and consequently create in the long run a worse state of things than that which they profess to remedy. The Christian who supports them proves thereby that he has not full confidence in the efficacy of his own system and his own Lord and Master. In other words, he has not faith. He helps in the self-deception of the unregenerate. He aids them in creating some fresh "fool's paradise."

Either this is true or else the very foundations of the Christian religion are wrongly placed; they are on sand and not on rock.

Sin is an endless circle—what the French call *le cercle vicieux*. Apart from divine, supernatural salvation, the history of mankind hitherto has been sin, war, death, and so on without end. Make a circle of these words and you will find it complete without a break. Fallen, unregenerate man can make no stopping place in the onward, self-producing course of sin. It would be as much opposed to law for him to do so as for water to run uphill. All his efforts to improve away his sins or those of his fellows but put commas, or at most semi-colons, in the endless circle.

At Calvary alone a full stop is put to sin. Christ entered the human family that He might join, as a sinless man, his sinful fellow-men in the endless circle. He brought righteousness, peace, life. They answered him with sin, war, death. But he rose again and broke the fatal circle. He opened "a way of escape" from the fateful "law" by first letting all the penalty thereof fall upon Him and exhaust its power in accomplishing His death. Thus each generation has presented to it the two alternative courses. The endless circle where sin seeks to be its own remedy—(so fittingly expressed by the pagan symbol of the serpent biting its own tail) or else the full stop at Calvary, where man is saved in ceasing thenceforth to be "his own" by becoming one body with his Lord, even as He became one flesh with our race for its salvation. There the blood is shed for sin once and for all. A full stop comes in the war-producing wars of men—for the law of sin and death has been fully "finished"; it has exhausted its claims upon the person of the Sinless One, and thenceforth (and at Calvary alone) starts a new cycle of life, a life which needs no swords or spears to protect it, a life of self -multiplying Christianity—for "the blood of the martyrs is the seed of the Church."

Here is the fateful circle—the endless cycle:

Sin > False Peace > War > Death . . . then a full stop at THE CROSS and then . . .**Purity > Peace > Life** . . . and thenceforth the endless circle of life for the glory of God, with its earthly expression in the holy war of salvation even, if needs be, unto the death of the Cross. This completed cycle of the Christian's career is beautifully summarized in the twelfth chapter of the Revelation: "and they overcame him (Satan) by the blood of the Lamb, and by the word of their testimony, and they loved not their lives unto the death." Beginning at the Cross in seeking their own salvation, they end at the Cross in seeking the salvation of others, and in sacrificing their lives in their turn in the holy war.

How absolutely opposite is, therefore, the war of Christianity to the wars of the world! How can these opposites possibly mingle? Must there not be something terribly wrong when they do ?

A quarter of a century of experience, in the most difficult forms of evangelistic war on the Continent of Europe, among five of its peoples, has steadily increased the conviction of the writer that war is a necessary part of the natural religion of fallen man. It is the red fruit which grows and ripens upon the tree of our so-called civilization, whose sap is essentially the same as in that of the civilization of the Babylonian, Medo-Persian, Grecian, or Roman empires. It is sin—though in a more cultivated, and therefore a more subtle and deceptive form. During a time of peace, the fruit develops quietly, sheltered and almost hidden by the plausible leaves of social respectability and international courtesy. But under the winds of some political autumn, the blood-red fruit falls. It is war, it commences a new cycle of sin, a new tree, which in its turn will bear fruit of the nature of the seed from which it sprang.

In the natural world apples are precisely the same in our day as in that of Nebuchadnezzar or of Nero. In the abnormal world of sin, its red war fruits are also of precisely the same nature as in the days of those kings. Its alliances, its "peace conferences," are also similar. Those empires passed away, leaving heaps of ruins. The result of their existence has been purely negative, so far as the redemption of mankind has been concerned. Among their ruins archaeologists spend their lives in deciphering pagan inscriptions, of which the greater part are records of bloody wars. Even in grammar two negatives destroy each other, and the sum total of all the results of all the destroying wars of mankind has been also—zero. This is equally true of their periods of peace. These increased the love of ease and the slothful licentiousness, which had been held in check by the brave and fierce occupations of war.

Peace alliances eventually led to fresh rents in the international fabric. Prosperity created enemies by arousing envy. Security engendered false confidence, peace conventions or negotiations false hopes. The zenith of the power and pride of earth's empires has ever coincided with the zenith of their folly and the hour of their fall.

At one moment it has been, "Is not this great Babylon, which I have built?" at the next they have fallen to earth to eat grass with the oxen and associate with the beasts of the field. Wherever religion has accompanied them in their course it has shared their fate; its exaltation has been its ruin; it, too, has become associated with the wild beasts of earth power, and has eaten their food as Nebuchadnezzar did, which is always a symptom of madness—of decent to a lower world. Human wars and peace, human pride and power thus always find their final expression in association with the brute creation and brute force. The blindness of fallen man is greater than that of the brute.

The Roman empire, at the divinely appointed time of our Lord's appearance as a babe at Bethlehem, embodied the nearest approach to universal rule ever attained before or since. And it crucified our Lord. It thus gave the exact measure of the blindness of these earth powers, whether pagan or nominally Christian. It demonstrated their true inwardness, and that of every religion which eats their food, shares in their glory, or supports their schemes of war or of peace. And when three centuries later the Roman Emperor, Constantine, exalted Christianity outwardly to a state religion, he only gave it a public certificate of inward declension. He inaugurated the dynasty of Christian religions, where the "harlot" sat upon "the beast," the false bride of Christ, enthroned in royal favour, and enjoying royal sustenance. In exchange for the sheathing of the spiritual sword Christianity shared the patronage of the carnal sword, and thenceforth "blessed" its enterprises.

That "history repeats itself" is thus not only the expression of a fact in the outward, but also in the inward world.

Never were the lessons of history carnal and history spiritual more necessary than in the present hour. We live in solemn days. The lines of demarcation between the kingdoms of this world and the kingdom of Christ are becoming effaced. The barriers between natural (fallen) and supernatural religion, between the invented and the revealed are being broken down. There are on all hands new theologies, which are in reality demonologies, for they repeat in some form or other Satan's lie, "the lie" of the Garden of Eden: "Ye shall be as God." They deny the deity of Christ: they make the first man in the street equally God with our blessed Lord. The consequence is that Christ's blood has no more efficacy to cleanse than that of any village carpenter of our day,—and therefore its shedding was equally meaningless as regards the making wars to cease.

The Scripture declaration that "peace is made by the blood of His Cross," and by it alone, is therefore false according to that theology. Thus there is no stop to war. The argument that men should not take life because they cannot give it back becomes futile. Every man is a god! And yet, were we to ask the theologians of this new school to perform a creative act, to create even a living flower as Christ created worlds, they would ridicule us for asking this proof of their equality with the Lord. Nor do they make men rise from the grave or ascend bodily to heaven as Christ did. It is because of the Christian's union with such a Saviour that war is so wrong. The only theology, therefore, which could make war right is the so-called "new theology" which affirms that He was but the son of Joseph. The representatives of war carnal and war spiritual are compromising their extreme claims, and meeting half-way in their peace conferences. Light is having fellowship with darkness, and "Christ" so-called with Belial. An intolerable confusion of ideas and principles is the result. Meanwhile all the profits of partnership go to the kingdom of darkness. On the one hand Christians are being befooled by the glittering wars of their nations, and the specious pleas by which they are justified, and on the other by their plausible schemes of peace. Here and there a shout of honesty cuts clean and clear through the confusion of tongues.

The President of a Republic honestly defends the policy of the "big stick": the Kaiser of an empire robustly advocates the philosophy of "the mailed fist"; meanwhile, pilgrimages of peace, in which Christianity is placed on the same footing as other religious systems, are the order of the day. The peace idea is momentarily popular. We may thus soon expect a proportionate swing of the pendulum to the other extreme as after the last Peace Conference.

Some huge European war must therefore be near at hand for: "When—they—say—peace and safety, then sudden destruction cometh upon them, as travail upon a woman with child!" And why? Because the wars of mankind have ever been formed in the womb of its peace, and come forth as suddenly as the apparent peace process was gradual and quiet. It is incredible that sane men should not see that like must ever produce like, and that every seed must produce a crop of its own kind. If men of war, armed to the teeth, plant a seed of peace, then Christ answers, "Every plant which My Heavenly Father hath not planted shall be rooted up!"

And all truly spiritual Christians echo the warning cry of their Master. The present hour thus demands of Christians a solemn re-examination of their whole position, and a more complete return to the forces, to all the forces of primitive, authentic Christianity.

If the humble effort represented by this book be of any service to one of the least and last of God's people in this respect, it will not have been made in vain.

Beyond that lowly hope the author has no interest. To no other system of reformation or of salvation, social or individual, could he afford to give a moment's thought. All the thinking powers and all the fighting forces of the last and the least of God's people are redeemed, bought up, monopolized, booked in advance, wholly and exclusively for the service of His kingdom! They dare not steal one of them for the service of world, flesh or devil, or their carnal systems of salvation. Salvation by the cross is their all-absorbing theme. The glory of their Lord is their all-mastering passion.

The object of this book is, therefore, to examine into the true inwardness of the wars and peace of the worldly, from the exclusive standpoint of Christianity. It is probable that both will be found to be absolutely non-Christian, and therefore anti-Christian, being essentially inspired by self-interest. The Scriptures affirm in a thousand forms that the unregenerate are incapable of any motives other than of a selfish order—and that all men high and low, "good" or bad, are equally "concluded under sin—except those living beyond the frontier line marked by the Cross of Christ, and in the new life of spiritual resurrection by living union with Him.

From many special causes the Continent of Europe seems to afford the best field for the study of this question. Out here, much more than in England, one comes to see how utterly "visionary," "impossible," and

even "absurd" the whole system and ethics of Christianity are to the men of this world. The truths which have become accepted in the British Isles as by common consent, such as salvation by faith, redemption by the blood of Christ—truths which it has not been hitherto fashionable to decry —are on the Continent accepted as the sure symptoms of hopeless fanaticism. One meets every day men who shrug their shoulders under a sense of sympathetic superiority, when in contact with those who actually believe in a God they have never seen, or in a Saviour who was crucified between two thieves by the high and sedate governments of the day—religious and political—as an object of their supreme scorn. What is the effect of such surroundings upon the living Christian?

Far from being discouraging, it is most invigorating. Accustomed to storms, like the pines on the Alpine heights, he learns to thrust his roots more firmly round the Rock of Ages. No sickly plants can live, much less thrive, in those solemn altitudes exposed to the wild whirlwinds, and on the edge of the beetling precipice. Down in the warm, cosy plains of English Christianity it is perhaps otherwise. Truth which costs little is generally valued proportionately little. In nations where the extremes of superstition and of militant infidelity have darkened the spiritual skies, the true Christian prizes the light of the gospel in all its forms to a proportionate degree. Not one aspect of truth can he forego.

He can engage in no kind of war than that of salvation, accept no other Prince of Peace than his Lord. He cannot be brought to value any kinds of man-made salvation. He can seek no favour from the earth powers which slew his Lord. In a heavy atmosphere, charged with doubt and materialism, where the hostile pressure upon every square inch of faith, so to speak—becomes incalculably great; in nations armed to the teeth, where the burden of taxation makes the masses live in a condition of sullen, bitter revolt—there Christians learn to find strength in the higher powers of the Cross, and in seeking to know and experience all that is for them in Christ Jesus. Especially in France you must fight for your life or sink down and die.

You must take the whole armour of God, or else be doubly exposed to the fiery darts of doubt, despair and defeat. You must become inseparably bound to Calvary by the bonds of an intense spirituality, and an unshakable loyalty to the cross, or else drift away on the current of secret doubt and despondency, and, like others before you, seek for help in a lower level, and by recourse to lower means.

CHAPTER SEVENTEEN

The Blood Tax

The Continent of Europe is, therefore, the best place in which to study the true inwardness of war carnal on the one hand, and war spiritual on the other.

As might have been expected, its special circumstances have combined to create before our very eyes an object lesson of the highest value, as a means of making the truth stand out with unparalleled clearness. Where sin abounds grace is seen much more to abound. The black background of sin, hatred and death at Calvary made righteousness, love and life stand out the more clearly. The very Cross lifted Jesus on high that all might behold Him. The extreme of the negative provides opportunity for the manifestation of the extreme of the positive.

Continental militarism has produced this result in a modern form. Here is its object lesson, and with it I conclude this book.

The conscription system prevailing on the Continent, by which every valid man must perform military service, brings out as nothing else can do the central truth of the Christian system for the conquest of the world for God: the blood tax. "Ye are not your own!" We almost hear the word spoken by the Continental rulers—that glorious, all-comprehensive word of Paul to his fellow-Christians. "Yes, you are not your own!"

"Ye are bought with a price." It was the price of the blood shed by ancestors or fellow-countrymen to extend or defend the Patrie or the Fatherland. "You owe a debt of blood to your land."

And what is this after all, but the exact and complete inversion of the greatest of all gospel truths: redemption by the blood. The doctrine which the worldly patriot limits to his one country and to the blood of multitudes of his forefathers shed for that one bit of land, the Christian extends to all countries and finds "fulfilled" and sufficiently expressed in the blood of one Man, one King—the Man, the King, his Lord, his Master!

Here once again we have the divine original standing out in perfect clearness and in complete contrast when placed over against the human counterfeit. Truth has an element of finality in it, error a non attaining, never-arriving, never-satisfying element. And here let me, at the risk of being misunderstood, affirm the settled conviction that the Continental doctrine of the blood tax is right and true doctrine for worldlings. It fits the facts. It is the only one corresponding to the reality. The Conscription System is supreme consistency. It is a doctrinal expression of one of the final necessities of society in a fallen world. Non-apostolic anti-militarism is deadly heresy, for it is supreme selfishness. Is a man then to enjoy in selfish ease the "liberty" purchased by the blood of others? Is he to refuse his life or blood, or that of his son, at the call of the fatherland to whom he owes all?

Blood was shed for me, and can I refuse to shed my blood for others? Nay, war is right. If you are a worldling you must practise worldliness, if you are honest. Its highest expression is war. Unless you have become dead to the world in the death of Christ and lost to the world by heavenly citizenship, then is it not mean, is it not cowardly, is it not selfish, to seek to escape military service? It is your duty to be faithful to your church, which is the world, and to your doctrines, which are worldliness, and to pay the blood tax in war. Are you not a thief and a traitor if you refuse? For you are not your own, you are bought with a price, you belong to your nation. Shall others go to fight your battles while you enjoy peace for worldliness, and a life of indifference towards the unspeakable woes under which our world groans? "No man liveth to himself." "We will not let him," says the Continental System. Nothing but an almost incredible ignorance of conditions prevailing upon the Continent could have led English statesmen to put forward the heretical doctrine of disarmament.

The German Emperor's disdain of the proposals simply proves once again that he is the most complete and representative type of honest worldliness at present prominently in public view on the grandstand of Gentile government. We fancy we can see him put his mailed fist to his face to hide a laugh. One can imagine one hears him saying: "You poor dear English statesmen with your Nonconformist conscience; in your island isolation you fancy you can have worldliness without war.

Absurdity! Your favoured position has blinded you to realities. I am a sceptic as regards worldly peace. I live on land. You live on water. This is what has led you into error. I have foreigners all around me whose land joins mine. You have foolishly allowed your statesmanship to become tainted with Christian peace heresies. They are all right for fools who are willing to die for Christ, an invisible King.

I am a visible one. I only accept as much Christianity as can be made to fit with my throne, court, ballrooms, and arsenals. Christianity, like all else, must serve my ends. Fire is good as a servant but objectionable as a master."

And all worldly powers do feel true Christianity to be fire! "I fear an idea more than an Army," said one Czar. Christianity does mean blood and a sword, for what is to be done with men who refuse to bear arms in war time? Military law allows them to be shot. And only when these its forces of blood and fire have become an empty name, can court Christianity exist. True Christianity is heresy to the worldly and their kings. "Worldliness is heresy to the true Christian and to his King. All that is required is for each to be true in his own sphere. "It is required of a steward that he be faithful."

The worldling must be true to blood-shedding principles and doctrines, the Christian to those of the Blood shed. Let this thought but get abroad in apostolic purity and definiteness, and it will help Christianity everywhere, by separating it from worldliness, and it will render a true service to worldliness by showing men that they must consent to and participate in bloodshed as long as they remain "their own" as unregenerate. Till they become converted and change into apostolic Christians the very Mood of Christ the King is on their hands every minute, every hour. Every second of their unsurrendered life they share in the crime committed at Calvary; then why should they scruple about shedding men's blood or employing the mightiest machines possible to that end in competition with other nations? Men who "crucify afresh" the King of Kings and "put Him to an open shame" by refusing to become His lowly, despised, unarmed followers.

Men who slay the very Author of Life, and stop up the channels of spiritual and eternal blessing at the fountain head—Calvary; why should they hesitate about the sacrifice of a few million human lives? It is here that the honest worldling is infinitely superior to the worldly Christian. One can understand men like M. Viviani, the French Minister, who with one sweep of his arm in the tribune of the French Chambers, cleared and cleaned the heavens of God, of hope, and of eternity, wiping out spiritual sun, moon, and stars at a stroke, as described in the Appendix—one can understand him advocating the Conscription System. He is logical.

"Ye are not your own!" You owe a blood tax to your cause ! You are blood bought ! And at what a price !

This is true of the Christian in the highest and fullest sense; and when he realizes that he owes to all his fellows all that he has received of God through the blood of Christ, then he will be gladly willing to pay the blood tax if need be, not as a soldier who kills, but as a missionary and a martyr. He will belong to humanity and not to any nation, and this will settle the question of war for him for ever.

But let the gilded youths of England, who live for themselves, beware ! Conscription may be not far off; it may claim them, though they have ignored the claims of Christ.

During a period of independent evangelistic work in recent years in Holland, I had occasion to speak on this question amongst converts and adherents. Some were led to adopt gospel peace principles. One young man, having been subsequently called up for military service, stood out from the ranks and told his officer he could not conscientiously bear arms, this being contrary to his convictions as a Christian. Immediately an anarchist called out from the ranks, "Bravo! I agree with you: I, too, am an anti-militarist."

"But I do not agree with you," was the reply, "you are an anarchist. Your principles are based on hatred and revolt; mine are just the opposite. You are for blood shedding; I will not fight because Christ shed His blood for me." Immediately many soldiers uttered exclamations of approval. The officer had momentarily given a little liberty of expression. He then spoke very kindly to the young Christian and told him he would remove him to infirmary work, and he did so. This incident illustrates "the great gulf fixed" between the two kinds of anti-militarism—the carnal and the spiritual, the worldly and the Christian.

Christians who refuse to bear arms on the Continent are exposed to false accusation, as in the days of the Roman Empire. They may be compared with revolutionaries or rebels.

The early Quakers had to suffer much on this account. They refused to take oaths on the principle that no Christian can act as if he had in use two kinds of truth-speaking, his oath being of a higher quality than his plain word—his affirmation. By their stand for the simplicity of truth (the "yea" and "nay" of which Christ said that "whatsoever is more than these cometh of the evil one"), they helped to win the present right which Englishmen enjoy, to affirm in the witness box instead of swearing—a liberty of which people of all denominations now make use. But the members of the Society of Friends had first to suffer terrible persecution for the above and similar reasons.

Hundreds were imprisoned for long periods and many died in jail. Their enemies profited by their conscientious scruples to wilfully confound them with treasonable characters under the following circumstances. As a test of loyalty to the king, an oath of allegiance was administered to all who came under the ban of the law for any reason, religious or criminal. The Quakers were among the number, through holding meetings in spite of adverse decrees. When they were brought up the oath was administered to them. On their refusal to swear, their enemies had the pretext they had sought for utterly crushing them.

The same confusing of principles will now be attempted. Hence the necessity for establishing a clear distinction, and for classifying the two opposing kinds of refusal to bear arms. The use of the bomb, the bullet, and the blade from above downwards seems to those beneath to justify their use upwards by their own hands.

Anarchy claims equal rights with autocracy. In Russia it is now a State within the State. It is a political party which claims to be the true exponent and administrator of "law" as towards the existing government above. There is a general breaking up going on everywhere. A world which has rejected the law of Calvary, the gospel, finds its own "laws" unavailing even for its own peace. And truly in final logic one is obliged to recognise that the only way to ascertain which party or political system is right is to judge them by their weapons. These are the same for all.

We therefore conclude that these earth powers are all one in spirit and nature, and that the Christian sins against the Christ when he takes up their weapons, that he gets the mark of the Beast in his forehead when he dons their helmets, kepis or caps, and that he gets the mark of the Beast in his hand when he grasps their weapons, whether it be the bayonet of autocracy or the bomb of anarchy. May we not legitimately see in the words of our King, "ye shall know them by their fruits," this application to present conditions: ye shall know them by their weapons? I am aware that to some I shall appear to tread on dangerous ground. All I ask is that they shall recognise that it is not political but Calvary ground. Let me ask any English objector this question: "In which party should a Christian bear arms in Russia at the present hour?" The majority of French and English sympathies are apparently with the anti-autocratic parties in that land. But that is practically the revolutionary party.

The English Premier's apostrophe: "The Duma is dead, long live the Duma !"was not politically colourless. And yet if the Scripture words, "honour the king," mean "bear arms for him," as the State Churches in all lands claim, how terrible is the position of isolation reserved for Russian Christians who happen to have republican views like, for instance, most Americans. And what would be their position if,—as often occurs in the ebb and flow of a civil war,— their village or town were alternately under imperial and republican governments, the authorities of the moment claiming their armed aid against the "enemy"? What would be their Christian duty? Two opposite answers involving life and death for them and their neighbours at each other's hands are demanded of them. Must not the only answer possible leap into view, as it were, between the two Beast forces of red autocracy and red anarchy, contending for the Christian's body via his soul? Fellow Christians! is it not the age-old answer of the brave Roman soldier Cassian, when he stood out from the ranks and cast his sword to the earth.

"I am a Christian, I cannot fight." Does not the whole situation remind us of the dilemmas in which Christ deliberately placed the rulers of the Jewish sects so often, that the common people might see what spirit they were of, that His was a different rule to theirs and that— blinded by carnal religion—they could not understand Him? They could not even see the Kingdom of God. Take, for instance. His question: "the baptism of John, was it from heaven or of men?" Immediately they were silent for political reasons. The Christ-man has no political reasons which can keep him silent. He is a Man of the cross, not of the sword. He is for the war which "is from heaven," and not that "which is of men," and entertains no Pharisaical considerations of political policy which could keep him from saying so.

The chief value of the study of the character of war is never to be found in the negative aspect, but in the view it gives, by contrast, of the real character and obligations of the true Christian warfare. That which is merely negative has no life in it. The question is not what war is wrong for Christians, but what war is right for them. It might be easy to proclaim the unlawfulness of war as an abstract principle, from a comfortable, quiet position, far removed from exposure to the dangers of any practical application of this doctrine, or from the fires of persecution, calumny, and loss which mark the fighting line of aggressive Christianity, face to face with hostile forces.

But when the proclamation of this truth is made in its normal atmosphere of conflict and suffering, as in the days of the early Quakers, for instance, then its true place in the Christian economy appears. It is an effect rather than a cause. It is one of the results of a spiritual state in which apostolic Christians, on fire with Divine Love, and constantly alive, through the inner light and power of the Holy Ghost, to the power of Christ to save their fellow-men, have no room for any thought of slaying them, or of even returning evil for evil. The wars of destruction would be as unnatural to them as would the war of salvation have been to the great warriors of history, the Alexanders, the Caesars, the Napoleons: the "war" of gospel missionary work. The spiritual drives out the carnal by a natural process. For the individual to put on peace principles as a cloak, or to accept them as a doctrinal legacy from ancestors, or from some particular denomination of Christians, without a corresponding intensity of divine war principles and practices, would be an anomaly. A truth, which is not personally experienced as life, is inoperative and self-deceiving. It has an element of unreality. It does not fit with facts. But the converse is also true: wherever there is a revival of the spirit of apostolic Christianity, there also appears a revival of the conviction and testimony that war is anti-Christian.

The breaking on all hands of the bonds uniting Church and State is significant. "War has always been bad for Christianity, and Christianity bad for war. Each has handicapped the other; each has hindered its unnatural associate, in the full development of his own character. It is to be hoped that the new era of the alliances between Pagan and "Christian" nations just opened by the treaty between England and Japan will help the disruption at home of all concordats and partnerships of the Cross and the sword, the Church and the State. Modern warfare harmonizes better with the principles of Shintoism and Buddhism, the chief religions of Japan, than with those of Christianity, and there is no doubt that if England were to adopt these religions instead of Christianity, it would be a great advantage to the prosecution of war. The awkward scruples of the Sunday School conscience would be effectually got rid of.

In another chapter of this book is shown the effort of the British Field Marshal to get rid of this very obstacle—Christian scrupulous truthfulness—in the interests of the untrammeled prosecution of bloody warfare.

One of the thoughts uppermost in the mind of the writer in issuing this volume is that we are now in the closing period of this Dispensation. The Scriptures clearly indicate that the end of the age would have a Laodicean character. The falling away from true faith would become more and .more rapid till the words would be fulfilled: "when the Son of Man cometh, shall He find faith on the earth?" (Luke 18:8), showing that our Lord was there speaking of the kind of faith which excludes all those false faiths under whose deluding influence our fallen race hopes to create in its own wisdom and power permanent peace and prosperity on earth. Gospel faith produces a hope of an exactly opposite character, namely one centered upon the return of the Lord.

It is the purifying hope alluded to in 1 John 3:3. As the end approaches the number of those whose life and conduct is governed by that hope will be ever smaller. The day of great revivals sweeping in large numbers of "converts" will have passed. Awakenings will be intensive rather than extensive. For in such times of stress the whole "Word of God will have to be believed and lived if men are to stand, and converts will have to take up their cross and be totally separated from the world from the start, as was the case with the early Christians. The current of the Apostasy will be overwhelmingly strong. One of the forms which the Purifying Hope must certainly assume is the entire removal of the spirit and views which have made participation in war and things associated with it still possible for those "born of the Spirit." May we each be true to our Lord and His truth at all costs. We owe to others all we have severally received from God.

The brief years of this final cleansing of the Spiritual Sanctuary may be nearer than we think, just as may be a revival of the fierce passions of war, leading to some European cataclysm of unprecedented magnitude.

Wherever we may stand in point of time, one thing is certain, that the Scriptures distinctly foreshadow, for the closing period of the Christian Era, the coming of a "tribulation" upon degenerate Christendom, far surpassing that which fell upon Judaism at the close of the Jewish Dispensation.

God's word to us all is "Be ye also ready!" May the trumpet of spiritual Christianity give no uncertain sound in those days, as to the true nature of the wars of the Beast-forces of this world, that everyone may, in the spiritual sphere, "prepare himself for the battle."

The Humanising of War

How far the Peace Conference of 1899 was successful in the task of making war more humane may be judged from the following:

THE NATAL WAR
REVOLTING DETAILS OF THE FIGHTING. A SOLDIER'S LETTER
Published in the Daily News, of August 16th, 1906

My dear Mamma, We have had several big fights, but the greatest day was a week on Sunday, when the rebels got such a cutting up that it was thought probable the affair was at an end.

We were called out of bed at two o'clock on Sunday morning, and reached our destination at daybreak.

You will have heard what a difficult task it is to get through the Zululand bush, and it is a great credit to all engaged when it is considered that no white man has ever been there before. Sigananda, one of the chiefs who was captured, and who is so old (107) and infirm that the officers have not yet made up their minds whether to shoot him or not, says we do not fight like our grandfathers did. Our forefathers would never have risked their lives so far as to penetrate into the bush after the rebels.

Just try to fancy walking through a place trellised with monkey creepers as tough as steel ropes, and so thick that you cannot see more than a yard before you. Besides this, the thorns, measuring from one to three inches, are everywhere, and it looked just as simple to walk through a

Blood Against Blood

granite wall. It was in one of these patches that we found the men we have been looking for so long, namely, "Sigananda," "Bambata," and "Madhlogozulu," and, of course, all their rebel followers. As quietly as possible they were surrounded in their rendezvous. The place was for all the world like a blind alley, shaped like a horseshoe, and open at the top. There were some three thousand of our men, and some got up above and round the entrance, while the remainder got in amongst our dusky brothers, as best possible.

Immediately the alarm was given all their fires were extinguished and Bedlam set loose. The firing lasted continuously for fifteen hours, and the noise of the Maxims and rifles commingled with the fiendish and unearthly shrieks of the natives was such that no pen or pencil could ever describe.

White Flag Fired On.

About nine o'clock am, Madhlogozulu (the paramount Chief "Demzulu's uncle") approached the Transvaal contingent, carrying a white flag. Some two or three hundred men accompanied him. He arrived a few yards in front of a sergeant, and explained that he wanted to give in. The reply, of course, was a bullet, that must have sent his brains some fifty yards off. His followers, who were now far too terrorized to use their weapons, stood back in a mass and shrieked for mercy. Mercy came quicker than expected—in the shape of a Maxim. What a sight! The whole bundle dropped lifeless in less than a minute.

Of course, the whole thing throughout was very repulsive, but orders are orders, and no man who showed himself escaped alive. Several women were among the slain, as well as a lot of young boys.

Several men came in and surrendered "Old Sigananda" was one of them; he was carried in on a litter, and had a shot through his foot. His two sons were with him, men between eighty and ninety years of age, and thirty or forty other followers. Most of them were shot next morning, but the old man and one or two more have still to meet their fate. The general way of dispatching the prisoners is to take them out of camp and tell

122

them to run away into the bush. They only get about twenty yards or so when a bullet reaches them, and, of course, it is "Good-bye, John" for them. I saw two shot one morning, and left where they fell. Next morning there was nothing left but their skeletons. So you see the birds make very fine scavengers, and it is always a big fine in Africa if you are caught shooting the carrion fowl.

Something arrived at the hospital tent that caused a pretty big commotion. It would, however, have caused a far greater commotion had it arrived in England. It was in a horse's nosebag, and the nigger who carried it seemed particularly anxious to get rid of it. It being addressed to the doctor, he was accordingly brought along, and the bag of mystery opened. Could you believe it, "Mamma"? It contained a man's head, and none other than "Bambata's." The story is a very pretty one, and quite fit for publication.

Kaffirs Left to the Vultures.

A few days previous a prisoner was captured and let go on the understanding that he brought news of where "Bambata" was, and while in pursuit of his research he struck Sunday's battlefield. I may here mention that the dead Kaffirs are left where they fall. There is no need to waste time burying the bodies, because the carrion fowl and any stray animals make short work of them in a day or two. Do you know that it only takes half a dozen of these birds a couple of hours to pick all the flesh off of a bullock ?

The faithful Kaffir was looking about among the fallen when he found "Bambata," and at once took steps to have his head brought into camp for identification. "Well, the first thing the doctor ordered was to have the matter kept secret, and also to have it stuffed at once. He had been struck with a Dum-Dum bullet on the back of the head, the bullet coming out of the left eye and carrying away half of the left jaw. His brains were gone more or less, but altogether we managed to get about three pounds of wool into his cranium, and afterwards placed the head in a basin of spirits.

Even here it is recognized how much the Government is against the present picnic, and such a piece of ancient barbarism could not be made public. Therefore I at once saw how valuable a photo of his head would be, and got hold of a camera, one of the only cameras in camp, and got one or two good photos. I was just making my way off when I met the owner of the camera, who wanted a snapshot himself. Out of my usual goodness of heart I went back and let him take one, but alas! the doctor put in an appearance, and deprived us of the camera. He told us he would give both camera and plates back, but we have never seen them since.

We carried the head with us for about a week, when it was dissected, and the skull will probably be made into a nice tobacco-jar for someone.

Curiously enough, I was never in better health, and altogether the food is splendid. In fact, I think it is the finest picnic I have ever been at.

OFFICIAL ATHEISM AND AGNOSTICISM IN FRANCE
From the "Review of Reviews" Leader, March, 1907

There has been so much comment upon the atheistic bias of the anti-clerical movement in France that it may be well to place on record the exact words used by the Socialist Minister, Viviani, in a speech placarded by the Chamber throughout all the communes of France. Mr. Booth-Clibborn writes:

The version given several weeks later in the Times by Sir A. Austin having been incomplete, I offer the following translation from the Official of November 9th, which lies before me. Alluding to the work of the Revolutions of 1798 and 1848, and the prolongation of their lines under the Third Republic, he says:

"Our forefathers, our fathers, and ourselves have unitedly continued hitherto a work of anti-clericalism and irreligion. "We dragged human consciences away from religious belief. "When a wretched creature, bending under his burdens, knelt to pray, we raised him up, we told him that there were no realities behind those clouds. Together, by a magnificent gesture, we extinguished in the heavens those lights which will never be relit. {Prolonged applause from the Left and Extreme Left.)

That is our work; it is our revolutionary work. Do not imagine it is ended; it is only beginning. It is surging upwards, it overflows us. And what can you reply to a man who is seeking justice here below, to a man who—thanks to us—is no longer a believer; to one whom we have snatched from the 'faith* and to whom we have declared that there was no justice in the heavens?"

Mr. Stead continues:

M. Briand, M. Viviani's colleague, subsequently disclaimed, on behalf of the Ministry, any desire on the part of the State to take sides in the great controversy of God or no God. The State, he maintained, was color-blind as to theological and anti-theological questions. That is no doubt the true attitude of the secular State. But the faith of men like Viviani in their atheistic creed is much too passionate to allow them to be neutral. Coleridge a hundred years ago described not only the phenomenon of Vivianism but its genesis:

"The sweet words Of Christian promise, words that even yet Might stem destruction, were they wisely preached, Are muttered o'er by men, whose tones proclaim How flat and wearisome they feel their trade: Rank scoffers some . . . The very name of God Sounds like a juggler's charm; and, bold with joy, Forth from his dark and lonely hiding place (Portentous sight!) the owlet Atheism, Sailing on obscene wings athwart the noon, Drops his blue-fringed lids, and holds them close, And hooting at the glorious sun in Heaven, Cries out, Where is it?" But nowadays the owlet, growing bolder, chortles gleefully, "We've put it out."

THE WORDS OF OUR LORD CONCERNING THE "TWO SWORDS."

Jonathan Dtmond in his *Essays upon Christian Morality* thus explains "He that hath no sword let him sell his garment and buy one." Luke 22:36

This is another passage that is brought against us. "For what purpose," it is asked, "were they to buy swords, if swords might not be used?" It may be doubted whether with some of those who advance this objection it is not an objection of words rather than of opinion. It may be doubted whether they themselves think there is any weight in it. To those, however, who may be influenced by it, I would observe that, as it appears to me, a sufficient answer to the objection may be found in the immediate context: " 'Lord, behold here are two swords,' said they; and He immediately answered, 'It is enough.' " How could two be enough when eleven were to be supplied with them? That swords in the sense, and for the purpose, of military weapons, were ever intended in this passage, there appears much reason for doubting. This reason will be discovered by examining and connecting such expressions as these: "The Son of Man is not come to destroy men's lives but to save them," said our Lord. Yet, on another occasion. He says, "I came not to send peace on earth, but a sword." How are we to explain the meaning of the latter declaration? Obviously, by understanding "sword" to mean something far other than steel.

There appears little reason for supposing that physical weapons were intended in the instruction of Christ. I believe they were not intended, partly because no one can imagine His apostles were in the habit of using such arms, partly because they declared that the weapons of their warfare were not carnal, and partly because the word "sword" is often used to imply "dissension," or the religious warfare of the Christian. Such a use of language is found in the last quotation; and it is found also in such expressions as these: "shield of faith," "helmet of salvation," "sword of the spirit," "I have fought the good fight of faith."

But it will be said that the apostles did provide themselves with swords, for on that same evening they asked, "Shall we smite with the sword?" This is true, and it may probably be true also, that some of them provided themselves with swords in consequence of the injunction of their Master. But what then? It appears to me that they acted on this occasion upon the principles upon which they had wished to act on another, when they asked, "Wilt thou that we command fire to come down from heaven, and consume them?" And that their Master's principles were also the same in both: "Ye know not what manner of spirit ye are of ; for the Son of Man is not come to destroy men's lives but to save them." This is the language of Christianity; and I would seriously invite him who now justifies "destroying men's lives," to consider "what manner of spirit he is of."

I think, then, that no argument arising from the instruction to buy swords can be maintained. This at least we know, that when the apostles were completely commissioned, they neither used nor possessed them. An extraordinary imagination he must have.

Who conceives of an apostle, preaching peace and reconciliation, crying "forgive injuries," "love your enemies," "render not evil for evil," and at the conclusion of his discourse, if he chanced to meet violence or insult, promptly drawing his sword and maiming or murdering the offender. "We insist upon this consideration. If swords were to be worn, swords were to be used and there is no rational way in which they could have been used, but some such as that which we have been supposing. If, therefore, the words, "He that hath no sword let him sell his garment and buy one," do not mean to authorise such a use of the sword, they do not mean to authorise its use at all: and those who adduce the passage must allow its application in such a case, or they must exclude it from any application to their purpose.

Upon the interpretation of this passage of Scripture, I would subjoin the sentiments of two or three authors. Bishop Pearce says, "It is plain that Jesus never intended to make any resistance, or suffer a sword to be used on this occasion." And Campbell says, "We are sure that He did not intend to be understood literally, but as speaking of the weapons of their spiritual warfare." And Beza: "This whole speech is allegorical. My fellow soldiers, you have hitherto lived in peace, but now a dreadful war is at hand; so that, omitting all other things, you must think only of arms. But when He prayed in the garden and reproved Peter for smiting with the sword. He Himself showed what these arms were."

Jonathan Dymond further says concerning the general principle:

"Of the injunctions that are contrasted with 'eye for eye, and tooth for tooth,' the entire scope and purpose is the suppression of the violent passions, and the inculcation of forbearance, and forgiveness, and benevolence, and love. They forbid, not specifically the act, but the spirit of war; and this method of prohibition Christ ordinarily employed. He did not often condemn the individual doctrines or customs of the age, however false or however vicious; but He condemned the passions by which only vice could exist, and inculcated the truth which dismissed every error. And this method was undoubtedly wise. In the gradual alterations of human wickedness, many new species of profligacy might arise which the world had not yet practised: in the gradual vicissitudes of human error, many new fallacies might obtain which the world had not yet held : and how were these errors and these crimes to be opposed, but by the inculcation of principles that were applicable to every crime and to every error?—principles which do not always define what is wrong, but which tell us what always is right."

EXTRACT PROM "THE ECCENTRICITY OF RELIGION."
By Henry Drummond.

"They said, He is beside Himself." Mark 3:21

We are confronted here with an episode in His life which is not included in any of these, an episode which had a bitterness all its own, and such as has fallen to the lot of few to know. It was not the way the world treated Him; it was not the Pharisees; it was not something which came from His enemies; it was something His friends did. When He left the carpenter's shop and went out into the wider life, His friends were watching Him. For some time back they had remarked a certain strangeness in His manner. He had always been strange among His brothers, and now this was growing upon Him. He had said much stranger things of late, made many strange plans, gone away on curious errands to strange places.

What did it mean? Where was it to end? Were the family to be responsible for all this eccentricity? One day it had culminated. It was quite clear to them now. He was not responsible for what

He was doing. It was His mind also that had become affected. He was beside Himself. In plain English, He was mad! An awful thing to say when it is true. A more awful thing when it is not; a more awful thing still when the accusation comes from those we love, from those who know us best.

Observe from the world's standpoint the charge is true. A holy life is either supernatural or morbid. For what is being beside one's self? What is madness? It is eccentricity—ex-centricity—having a different centre from other people. Now, when Jesus Christ came among men He found them nearly all revolving in one circle. There was but one centre to human life—self. Man's chief end was to glorify himself and enjoy himself for ever. His object in going about was not gain but to do good. Now, all this was very eccentric. It was living on new lines altogether. He did God's will. He pleased not Himself. His centre was to one side of self. He was beside Himself. From the world's viewpoint it was simply madness.

Think of this idea of His, for instance, of starting out into life with so quixotic an idea as that of doing good; the simplicity of the expectation that the world ever would become good, this irrational talk about meat to eat that they knew not of, about living water; these extraordinary beatitudes, predicating sources of happiness which had never been heard of; these paradoxical utterances of which He was so fond, such as that the way to find life was to lose it, and to lose life in this world was to keep it to life eternal. What could these be but mere hallucination and dreaming? It was inevitable that men should laugh and sneer at Him. He was unusual. He would not go with the multitude, and men were expected to go with the multitude. What the multitude said, thought and did were the right things to have thought, said or done, and if anyone thought, said or did differently his folly be on his own head. He was beside Himself, He was mad.

The servant is not above his master. If they have persecuted me they will also persecute you. A Christian must be different from other people. Time has not changed the essential difference between the spirit of the world and the spirit of Christ. They are radically and eternally different. And from the world's standpoint still Christianity is eccentricity. For what, again, is Christianity? It is the projection into the world of these lines along which Christ lived. It is a duplicating in modern life of the spirit, the method and the aims of Jesus, a following through the world the very footprints He left behind. And if these footprints were at right angles to the broad beaten track the world went along in His day, they will be so still. It is useless to say the distinction was broken down.

These two roads are still at right angles. The day may be, when the path of righteousness shall be the glorious highway for all the earth. But it is not now. Christ did not expect it would be so. He made provision for the very opposite. He prepared His church beforehand for the reception it would get in the world. He gave no hope that it would be an agreeable one. Light must conflict with darkness, truth with error.

There is no sanction or place in the world for a life with God as its goal, and self- denial as its principle. Meekness must be victimized; spirituality must be misunderstood; true religion must be burlesqued. Holiness must make a strong ferment and reaction, in family or community, office or workshop, wherever it is introduced.

"Think not that I am come to send peace on the earth. I came not to send peace but a sword." Paul tells us the charge was laid at his door. He had made that great speech in the hall of the Caesarean palace before Agrippa and Festus. He told them of the grace of God in his conversion, and closed with an eloquent confession of his Lord. "What impression had he made upon his audience? The impression of a madman, "As he thus spake for himself, Festus said with a loud voice, Paul, thou art beside thyself; much learning hath made thee mad." Poor Paul! How you feel for him when the cruel blow was struck.

But there was no answer to it. From their view it was perfectly true. And so it has been with all saints to the present hour. It matters not if they speak, like Paul, words of soberness. It matters not if they are men of burning zeal like Xavier and Whitfield.

It applies to inventors, discoverers, to philosophers, to poets, to all men who have been better or higher than their times. These men are never understood by their contemporaries. And if there are martyrs of science, the centres of science being in this world, seen, demonstrated, known, how much more must there be martyrs for religion, whose centre is beyond the reach of earthly eye! The more active religion is the more unpopular it must be. Christ's religion did not trouble His friends at first ; for thirty years, at all events, they were con-tent to put up with it.

But as it grew in intensity they lost patience. When He called the twelve disciples, they gave Him up. His work went on, the world said nothing for some time. But as His career became apparent more and more, the family feeling spread, gained universal ground. Even the most beautiful and tender words He uttered were quoted in evidence of His state. For John tells us that after that exquisite discourse in the tenth chapter about the Good Shepherd, there was a division among the Jews for these sayings: "And many of them said, he hath a devil and is mad. Why hear ye him?" It seemed utter raving.

Signal Lights

On our Continental railways, one sees when approaching a terminus, ground signals consisting of large white letters painted upon black, and upon which a powerful hooded lamp placed with its back to the arriving train, projects a beam of light, making the signal stand out in startling relief amid the surrounding darkness. The group of letters one most frequently sees is B I F U R— bifurcation. It marks a "point," and the changing of the ways. Here there is sometimes a momentary halt, and then, perhaps in answer to an appealing whistle, the point is opened, the train is switched onto the right line, and enters the terminus safely. Similes drawn from nature or art can only incompletely illustrate spiritual truths. Yet we have here one which may, with sufficient aptness, resume the object of the biographical details offered to the reader in the following section.

What is the word which, for the Christian, stands out in the darkness at every crisis, at every parting of the ways, at every bifurcation? It is a word of the same number of letters; it is JESUS. It is the pure white NAME on the black ground of sin. The "points" are Calvary. To shed light on the cross is the one thing God asks of the Christian, for it is the only one by which he can be of any service to his fellows. Like the lantern whose back is carefully covered that it may not obtrude itself upon the view and thus obscure the signal, but concentrate and project the light all the more powerfully upon the one object of supreme importance in the surrounding darkness, so the Christian directs all his undivided energies to making the NAME that is above every name stand out before men. For this work and for this alone, he is assured of the help of the Holy Spirit. Help is not even the word. He but offers himself to the Spirit as an instrument through which He can cast His divine light upon the Cross, and the work of the world's Redeemer. This is why the Spirit of God ever gives the Christian such a hatred of anything which could uselessly draw attention to himself, or make him all unwillingly obstruct the view of his Lord. He is filled with a holy jealousy for the Truth and a passionate desire that every eye be directed upon the Saviour, and every faculty engaged in the contemplation of that ONE source of salvation and wisdom.

This is doubly so because the very work of the Holy Spirit Himself is to shed light upon the person of the ever-living Christ and His work upon Calvary. "He shall testify of Me," said our Lord.

Our duty and privilege as reflectors, destined to make the face of Jesus appear in the world's darkness, is beautifully expressed in a French version of 2 Corinthians 4:6

> **"For God who commanded 'let the light shine in the darkness,' has made the light shine in our hearts in order to make the knowledge of the glory of God shine upon the face of Jesus."**

The work of the fallen spirit of man has ever been the exact opposite. He sheds light upon mere man. He glorifies man. Man is his hope, his god. Never was there such an effort to obtain symposiums of the opinions of men on any question.

The moral and spiritual views of men of all religious beliefs or disbeliefs are collated to form one common combination of "wisdom." This is an anti-Christian disposition. The work of the fallen spirit of men has ever been to make earthly heroes and redeemers.

Thus the good to be derived from the life and testimony of Christians, men or women of the past, is in exact proportion to the light which they shed—not upon themselves, but upon Christ.

This is the object I have in view in the following brief biographical notices. Let these servants of God be here what they wished to be when living: but a lamp with a shade and a covered back in which the men of the world saw "no beauty that they should desire" them, but which thus attained their one object all the more faithfully: to throw light upon the beloved face of their Master. To this alone would the writer of these lines also aspire. Let the faults or imperfections of this effort be thus lost sight of in its object to join his readers in an inquiry as to the lawfulness of war by making the face of Christ, the work of Calvary, and the blood of the Cross shine out in the darkness.

Two Wars Two Warriors

Towards the middle of the seventeenth century and almost in the same year (1655-6) two military men became Christians by the new birth, and as a consequence, saw war to be wrong for them. They renounced it as being a form of worldliness, and advocated peace by righteousness. Thenceforth worldliness was at war with them.

One was Colonel David Barclay, of Ury, Scotland, who had served under Gustavus Adolphus. Among his descendants were Joseph John Gurney (the coworker of Wilberforce) and his sister, Elizabeth Gurney Fry, whose respective labours among and on behalf of prisoners and slaves were greatly blessed of God a century and a half later.

The other was John Clibborn, of Cliborne, Durham, who served under Oliver Cromwell, went with him to Ireland, and established himself there.

Both were my ancestors. Their lives are links—on the plane of human instrumentality and spiritual legacy—connecting these pages with the teaching and example of primitive Christianity.

The powerful religious awakening, under which these two men were brought to Christ, and from courageous service in carnal war to even more fear- less devotion in spiritual war, has been called "the great revival of the latter half of the seventeenth century." The people used of God in this mighty movement were named in derision Quakers, because they told sinners to tremble at the thought of their sins, of a holy God and of the doom of the impenitent. The work and teaching of George Fox and the "Society of Friends," the terrible sufferings inflicted upon these true Christians, and their

137

sublime constancy, require no more than a bare allusion here. A few striking incidents bearing upon the subject of this book which occurred in the lives of the two men in. question, I will now relate in this connection.

The following account of the constancy under trial of one of them is taken from *"Six Generations of Friends in Ireland,"* by J. M. R.

"John Clibborn was an officer in Cromwell's army, and a man of strong character and considerable local influence. "About the year 1658, when twenty-six years of age, he came with the Army of the Parliament into Ireland, and settled on a property in Moate, King's County. His descendants still inhabit Moate Castle, the family seat.

"John Clibborn had a great aversion to the people called Quakers, and finding that they had a Meetinghouse on his land, he determined to clear them off by burning this house. Provided with fire he went to the place, when, as he supposed, it was empty, but to his surprise he found a meeting going on, and Thomas Lowe preaching. He threw away the fire, sat down behind the door, and became so powerfully affected that his purpose was immediately changed. On his return home, his wife asked if the Quaker Meetinghouse was burned.

'No,' said he. 'If you will come to meeting there next Sunday and do not like it, I will go with you to church the following Sunday.' "She accordingly went, and Thomas Lowe again preached. Both joined the Friends, and John Clibborn built a Meeting-house, which, with a burial ground, he bequeathed to the Society for ever.

"He was of a generous, open-hearted disposition, beloved and esteemed in his neighbourhood, very hospitable, especially to strangers who came on errands of love, preaching the Gospel of Peace.

"His situation in the Civil "Wars, during the struggle of James II to retain his power, was very perilous, as his house was only a few miles from Athlone, where the Irish Army had established their garrison, and from whence issued parties to distress the country. (1689.)

"Meetings were kept up at great hazard. Succouring many, and endued with Christian love, John Clibborn held on his way in patience and courage. He was one night dragged by his hair from that home which had been long a refuge for the distressed, but which was now the spoil of the plunderer, and in flames.

"His life was attempted three times by the blood thirsty foes around him, and at last they laid his head on a block, and raising the hatchet, prepared to strike the fatal blow. He called for a brief respite, and then knelt down to pray, as did Stephen, that the sin might not be laid to their charge. Just then another party arrived, and asked: 'Who have you got there?' and were answered: 'Clibborn.' 'Clibborn!' they echoed, 'a hair of his head shall not be touched.'

"Escaping with his bare life, almost naked, he wrapped a blanket around him and presented himself before the Commander at Athlone. "The officer desired him to point out the men who had been guilty of this outrage, and they should be hanged before his hall-door. But he refused, saying he bore them no ill-will, and only desired that his neighbours and himself might be allowed to live un- molested.

"John Clibborn lived to see tranquillity restored, and ended in peace his long life in 1705."

It was under the ministry of the Thomas Lowe mentioned in this narrative that William Penn, sub-sequently founder of Pennsylvania, was led to Christ and to the adoption of the principles of the Society
of Friends.

David Barclay had fought beside Gustavus Adolphus when he fell at Lutzen, in 1632. He was descended from a family (de Berkeley) which had since the time of the Norman Conquest given many military men to the Scottish wars. Colonel David Barclay was at one time military governor of all Scotland north of the Tay. He came under conviction of sin, and began to seek Christ. During a time of imprisonment in Edinburgh Castle consequent upon political upheavals, he received much spiritual blessing from a fellow-prisoner. Lord Swintonne (an ancestor of Sir "Walter Scott), of whom it was said that "during his imprisonment he seemingly cared more for spreading Christian truth than for defending his own life. "After experiencing the new birth Colonel Barclay renounced war as anti-Christian and suffered imprisonment and much persecution in consequence. He had fallen into "the scandalous errors of Quakerism," according to the Presbytery of the diocese of his brother-in-law, Bishop Strachan.

The American poet Whittier, in a note appended to his poem describing an incident in the life of David Barclay, says:

"As a Quaker, he became the object of persecution and abuse at the hands of the magistrates and the populace. None bore the indignities of the mob with greater patience and nobleness of soul than this once proud gentleman and soldier. One of his friends, on an occasion of uncommon rudeness, lamented that he should be treated so harshly in his old age who had been so honoured before. 'I find more satisfaction,' said Barclay, 'as well as honour, in being thus insulted for my religious principles, than when, a few years ago, it was usual for the magistrates, as I passed the city of Aberdeen, to meet me on the road and conduct me to public entertainments in their hall, and then escort me out again, to gain my favour."

His son Robert became a leading Quaker theologian. He had made his theological studies in a Roman Catholic college in Paris, of which his uncle was rector. Converted at nineteen during silent prayer in a Quaker meeting, he published "Barclay's Apology" at 28. It helped to diminish persecution, though not to the extent attributed to it by Voltaire. There were 4,200 "Friends" in prison at one time. Hundreds died there. Robert Barclay travelled in gospel service with George Fox and William Penn. After one of their visits to Holland, Barclay wrote and presented a powerful appeal in Latin to the Powers about to assemble for a Peace Conference at Nimeguen (1677). It showed that war was anti-Christian and that peace could never be made in the world except by regeneration, and as a result of vital Christianity.

To show how complete and clear-sighted through being firmly established upon Christian conviction was the renunciation of the world, its honours and its wars, made by young Robert Barclay, it may be mentioned that his mother,—daughter of Sir Robert Gordon, of Gordonstown,—came of a warlike race, whose leaders, women, as well as men, had caused much blood to be shed, and had experienced the vicissitudes of political fortune.

In his godly mother's life, in his own powerful advocacy of the double truth that the carnal war is wrong and unlawful for Christian men, and spiritual war, as evangelists and missionaries, right and lawful for Christian women, he helped to re-establish at a stroke the principles of primitive Christianity in both these aspects so closely connected.

Not till 200 years after Christ, when war first began to be looked upon as right, did woman's ministry begin to disappear. Is it not the natural conclusion that with the disappearance of the wrong "ministry" for Christian men—war, there should reappear the right of women to share publicly in the right war?

Again, in the eighteenth century, our family was put to terrible test and endured much loss of property during the Irish Rebellion rather than take up arms. When the insurrection was brewing the members of the Society of Friends in Ireland destroyed all their guns and fowling pieces as an act of obedient faith to God. The "Quakers are mad," said people of all classes, religious and worldly, as the frightful scenes of carnage began to redden the land with blood and fire. Yet though their lives were frequently threatened, they were marvelously preserved. Their homes became a place of refuge for combatants of both parties and their wives.

The "Friends" went regularly to their raeetings, even the week-day ones, though in one or two cases they had to remove the dead bodies from the road that their conveyances might pass. Their fearless example of faith and perseverance in thus putting God first in everything had blessed results upon their neighbours, and contributed to their personal safety, though it had appeared at first as if they were unnecessarily exposing themselves. Faith and calculation are often mutually excluding.

The remarkable fortitude of the women Friends doubtless found part of the source of its strength in their position in the Society. While family relationships were maintained in the divine order, mothers and daughters were expected to be warriors for Christ and to obey the Spirit in public ministry as called of God.

As I am dealing especially here with ancestral examples, which subsequently affected both my views and duties in this question of the two opposite kinds of war, the carnal and the spiritual, I shall briefly refer to some who were prominent women ministers in the Society. Little do those who seem to fancy religious conviction can be easily sacrificed or surrendered on such points as the one in question, and who have not had such examples standing out in line across centuries in their own family, little can they understand how unshakable is the conviction they produce. It is solemn beyond words. Those fore fathers and mothers have joined the great cloud of witnesses.

Cowper said: "My boast is not that I derive my birth From loins enthroned or rulers of the earth: But higher far my proud pretensions rise, The child of parents passed into the skies." Among these, in the latter part of the eighteenth century, was Margaret Shackleton, a devoted minister of the Society. During the fearful scenes of the rebellion she "endured as seeing Him who is invisible," and had faith through all for the dear children gathered under her care. Her grandfather, Abraham Shackleton, of Ballitore, had left her a noble example.

In his book, Peace Principles, Dr. Hancock, speaking of the same homestead, says: "During the Irish Rebellion, Colonel "Wolseley and his lady, the wives of two lieutenants, also the wives of two privates, and a sick soldier were protected under his roof while their enemies had possession of the town." He describes how by Abraham Shackleton's (junior) staunch adherence to peace principles, at the risk of his life,—as the tides of war ebbed and flowed around,—his neighbours, rich and poor, and persons of all parties, a hundred in all, sheltered peacefully under his roof. He and his family were in constant danger. His home was invaded by riotous . savage insurgents one day, and the next in danger of the loyalist cannon. He was even taken out "to stop a bullet as he would not fight."

After the English victory, "he and his colleagues in the work of peace continued to interpose their good offices, when judicial proceedings were gleaning the refuse of the sword ; and had the satisfaction of contributing to save many of their neighbours from death. A man who was tried by a court-martial ascribed his acquittal to a note in his favour by A. Shackleton's sister. The officer glanced at the signature, and remarked that it was from a Quaker, and that Quakers never lie."

The officer presiding over the council was Colonel Colin Campbell

Seeing that such were the experiences of those officers in connection with my ancestors,—plain Christians of the primitive kind—I may be acquitted of any charge of taking too great liberty in my impartial analysis of Viscount Wolseley's doctrine. The Colonel Wolseley above named was of the same family, and, if I am rightly informed, his great uncle.

When the Quakers principles of peace have not been on fierce trial in time of war, the ideal held before Friends by many courageous self-denying examples has been that of the holy war of salvation carried abroad. What more blessed fact could be recorded on the pages of history than that which is often lost sight of amid the stories of conquest and carnage with which school books are stained on every page—that for seventy years the Quakers lived among savage tribes in Pennsylvania absolutely unarmed, that they never lost a faithful member at the hands of the savages, even when fierce struggles raged around?

During the last fifty years the Society of "Friends" has laboured in the evangelistic and missionary field with renewed energy and consecration.

A beautiful memory which stands out in my childhood is that of distributing prospectuses in Ireland for public meetings for that man of God—Jonathan Grubb. I can still remember the glow of his soul. He laid his hand on my head and said he believed God would call me to the ministry. This was fulfilled when at an unusually early age, the Society of Friends in the north of Ireland "recorded" me a minister. Among "Friends" no minister is "made" they "acknowledge" after perhaps years of waiting and spiritual testing, those whom they believe God has made ministers. I have therefore always looked upon this acknowledgement as involving much responsibility as regards faithfulness to spiritual religion and Christian principle. When called in 1881 by divine proveniences and by the urgent invitation of the heads of the Salvation Army, to the career of a foreign missionary in France and Switzerland, whose languages I had acquired at school in the lat-ter country, I stated that I could never forego any of the essential truths of Quakerism, and I entered the work on that understanding.

Mrs. Booth felt at The time considerably drawn towards those views, and read Barclay's "Apology" with deep interest and fellowship of spirit. It is my deep conviction that had she been alive during the last decade and face to face with its great military developments, and of threatening conscription in England, she would have agreed with the main lines of this book, and also with the definite stand taken by her eldest daughter Catherine, my dear wife, on this question at the time of the Anglo-Dutch War.

I believe that with the restoration of women's ministry to its normal place in the public service of Christ, the unlawfulness of war for the Christian will become ever more evident.

But more stimulating than all this testimony from the seventeenth and eighteenth centuries has been the fact that when it continued on into the nineteenth it began to be overlapped by another and perhaps the most confirmatory of all, so far as this present effort is concerned.

foundationuniversitypress.com

ti

www.ingramcontent.com/pod-product-compliance
Lightning Source LLC
Chambersburg PA
CBHW020255130626
46549CB00005B/2221